THE PROPERTY INVESTORS MANAGEMENT HANDBOOK

DAVID WATSON

EMERALD PUBLISHING
WWW.STRAIGHTFORWARDCO.CO.UK

Emerald Publishing
Brighton BN2 4EG

ISBN 1903909 99 6

Printed by Webspeedbooks Bedfordshire
www.webspeedbooks.com

Cover design by Straightforward Graphics

CONTENTS

Introduction

....

PART 1 - Buying A Property

....

1. **Purchasing a property for investment**   **11**
   The budget   11
   Deposits   11
   Stamp duty   12
   Other conveyancing costs   12
   Land registry   13
   Searches   13
   Structural surveys   13
   Mortgage fees   15
   Mortgage arrangement fees   15
   Advice for the investor-Letting out Property   15
   The importance of having a clear business plan   15
   What kind of property is suitable for letting?   16
   The business plan   17
   Main points from chapter 1   21

2. **Looking for a Property**   **23**
   Area   23
   Choosing your property   24
   Purchasing a flat   25
   Leasehold Reform Act 1993   26
   Viewing properties   26
   Buying a listed building   27
   Buildings in conservation areas   28
   Buying a new house   28

Building guarantees 29
Main points from chapter 2 31

3. The process of buying a property **33**
Making an offer 33
Exchange of contracts 34
Completing a sale 34
Buying a property in an auction 35
Preparing for auction 35
Buying before auction 36
At the auction 36
Sale by tender 36
Main points from chapter 3. 38

PART 2 – Letting the Property

4. Finding a tenant **41**
Letting agents 42
Advertisements 44
The public sector 44
Company lets 45
Short lets 46
Students 47
The DSS and housing benefit 48
Holiday lets 48
Bedsits 49
Showing the property to the tenants 50
Main points from chapter 5. 52

5. What should be provided under the tenancy **53**
Furniture 53
Services 54
Repairs 55
Insurance 55

At the end of the tenancy   55
Main points from chapter 5   57

....

PART 3 – Letting Property, The Law

....

6.   Managing property-the law   59
Explaining the law   59
The freehold and the lease   60
Freehold   61
Leasehold   61
The position of the tenant   61
The tenancy agreement   62
The contract   62
The responsibility of the landlord   64
  to provide a rent book
Overcrowding   65
Different types of tenancy agreement   65
The assured tenancy agreement   65
Other types of agreement   66
The squatter   66
Main points from chapter 6.   68

7.   Assured tenants   71
The assured tenant   71
The assured shorthold tenancy   71
Security of tenure   74
Grounds for possession of a tenancy   75
Fast track possession   80
Joint tenants. The position of two or more   80
people on a tenancy
Key points from chapter 8.   82

8.	**The right to quiet enjoyment of a home**	**83**
	Eviction-what can be done against unlawful harassment of a Tenant	83
	What can be done against unlawful eviction	85
	The injunction	85
	Damages	85
	Main points from chapter 10.	87
9.	**Going to court to regain possession**	**89**
	Applying for possession	89
	Main points from Chapter 14	92
10.	**Repairs and improvements**	**93**
	Repairs and improvements generally	93
	Examples of repairs a landlord is responsible for	94
	Reporting repairs to a landlord	95
	Tenants rights whilst repairs are being carried out	95
	Repairs and rent	96
	Tenants rights to make improvements to a Property	96
	Disabled tenants	96
	Shared housing-HMO's	97
	Sanitation health and hygiene	99
	Renovation grants	100
	Main points from chapter 11	102

....

PART 4 Rent, Service Charges and Income tax

....

11.	**Rent**	**105**
	The payment of rent and other matters	105
	The assured tenant	105
	Rent control for assured tenants	106

Council tax 106
Who has to pay council tax? 107
Dwellings that are exempt 107
Reductions in council tax bills 108
Benefits available to those on low incomes 108
Service charges 108
Deposits 110
Main points from chapter 10. 111

12. Income tax and benefit. **113**
Exemptions from income tax 113
Deductions from tax 114
Payment of benefit direct to the landlord 114
Housing benefit and possession for arrears of rent 115
Main points from chapter 11 116

13. Private tenancies in Scotland **117**

14. Advice for the tenant **125**

Glossary of terms
Index

Appendix 1. Example residential tenancy agreement
Appendix 2. Sample notice requiring possession
Appendix 3. Tenancy agreement (Scotland)
Appendix. 4. Notice requiring possession (Scotland)
Appendix 5. Household Inventory

INTRODUCTION

In the main this book is intended for the investor but can also be used by those who wish to gain a background in property management generally. It is estimated that, by 2020, half of all properties in the UK will be second homes or buy-to let. Demand in the buy-to-let sector will increase because housing supply will not keep up with demand. Mortgages are easier to obtain, fuelling the growth in this sector.

However, a note of caution!

If you are thinking of investing in a property for let, and you have had either no experience, or very little experience of the world of property and property management then you will find yourself suddenly involved in the complexities of the law of landlord and tenant.

Many people who invest in property do so without the slightest idea of the law and, quite often, come unstuck. This is particularly the case if you decide to carry out your own management, rather than let an agency handle it for you.

The first part of this book deals with the mechanics and the economics of purchasing a property, what costs are involved and where to buy.

The second part deals with the finding of a tenant. One of the main reasons for investing in property is to yield a long-term rental income and also to see capital growth. Therefore, finding a tenant, the right tenant, is of the utmost importance. There are many stories of would be landlords who spend a lot of time and trouble purchasing property, taking out large mortgages, only to come to grief when letting the property to someone who is totally irresponsible and doesn't pay rent.

The third part deals with the income tax obligations and the nature of the tenancy agreement. The fourth part deals with repairs and maintenance and also the right of the landlord to purchase the freehold or leasehold of the property that he or she has invested in. This book, the Property Investors Management Handbook will prove invaluable to all who read it.

Good luck!

PART 1

BUYING A PROPERTY

1

PURCHASING A PROPERTY
FOR INVESTMENT

In chapters 1, 2 and 3 we will look at the process of purchasing a property for investment. Although many of the processes are the same whether you buy for your own personal residence or for investment, i.e. to let, there are also fundamental differences which are covered in the second part of chapter one, the importance of having a clear business plan and having a clear idea of what types of property are suitable for letting.

In chapter 2 we look at the importance of looking for a property and the key elements that will be of interest to an investor. In chapter 3 we look at the actual process that an individual will go through when making the actual purchase.

Budget
Before beginning to look for a house or flat for investment you need to sit down and give careful thought to the costs.

Deposit
Sometimes the estate agent will ask you for a small deposit when you make the offer. This indicates that you are serious

about the offer and is a widespread and legitimate practice, as long as the deposit is not too much. £100 is usual.

The main deposit for the property, i.e., the difference between the mortgage and what has been accepted for the property, isn't paid until the exchange of contracts. Once you have exchanged contracts on a property the purchase is legally binding. Until then, you are free to withdraw. The deposit cannot be reclaimed after exchange.

Banks will normally lend up to 85% of the purchase price of the property for buy to let. However, the less you borrow, the more favorable terms you can normally get from bank or building society.

Stamp duty

Stamp duty is a tax paid on a property 1% between £125,000 and £250,000. The duty is 3% of purchase price between £250,000 and £500,000 and 4% for properties costing more than £500,000, which adds a significant amount to the conveyancing costs. If the house or flat costs £125,000 or under, no duty is payable, it is payable from £125,001 onwards.

Other conveyancing costs

A solicitor normally carries out conveyancing of property. However, it is perfectly normal for individuals to do their own conveyancing. All the necessary paperwork can be obtained from legal stationers and it is executed on a step-by-step basis.

It has to be said that solicitors are now very competitive with their charges and, for the sake of between £200-300 it is better to let someone else do the work which allows you to concentrate on other things.

Land Registry

The Land Registry records all purchases of land in England and Wales and is open to the public and also online (inspection of records, called a property search) The registered title to any particular piece of land or property will carry with it a description and include the name of owner, mortgage, rights over other persons land and any other rights. There is a charge for inspection. A lot of solicitors have direct links and can carry out searches very quickly. Not all properties are registered although it is now a duty to register all transactions.

Searches

These are checks with the local authority and other bodies, which ascertain whether or not there are any proposed developments or other works in the vicinity of the property which could jeopardize the value of the property in the future or the well being of the occupants.

There is normally a pro forma used for this as the questions are standard and a charge of between £60-£125 will be incurred.

Structural surveys

The basic structural survey is the homebuyer's survey and valuation, which is normally carried out by the building society or other lender. This will cost you between £100-150 and is not really an in-depth survey, merely allowing the lender to see whether they should lend or not and how much they should lend. Sometimes, lenders keep what they refer to as a retention, which means that they will not forward the full value (less deposit) until certain defined works have been carried out.

If you want to go further than a homebuyers report then you will have to instruct a firm of surveyors who have several survey types, depending on how far you want to go and how much you want to spend. However, after June 2007, it will be mandatory for all sellers to provide a sellers pack to potential purchasers, part of which will consist of a structural survey, although this part of the pack may be dropped.

A word of caution. Many people go rushing headlong into buying a flat or house. If you stop and think about this, it is complete folly and can prove very expensive later. A house or flat is a commodity, like other commodities, except that it is usually a lot more expensive. A lot can be wrong with the commodity that you have purchased which is not immediately obvious. Only after you have completed the deal and paid over the odds for your purchase do you begin to regret what you have done.

The true price, true market price of a property is not what the estate agent is asking, certainly not what the seller is asking. The true market price is the difference between what a property similar to the one in good condition is being sold at and your property minus cost of works to bring it up to that value.

Therefore, if you have any doubts whatsoever, and if you can afford it anyway, get a detailed survey of the property you are proposing to buy and get the works required costed out. When negotiating, this survey is an essential tool in order to arrive at an accurate and fair price. Do not rest faith in others, particularly when you alone stand to lose.

One further word of caution. As stated, a lot of problems with property cannot be seen. A structural survey will highlight those. In some cases it may not be wise to proceed at all.

Mortgage fees

Mortgage indemnity insurance. This is a one-off payment if you are arranging a mortgage over 70-80% of lenders valuation. This represents insurance taken out by the lender in case the purchaser defaults on payments, in which case the lender will sell the property to reclaim the loan. It is to protect the mortgage lender not the buyer.

The cost of the insurance varies depending on how much you borrow. A 90% mortgage on a £60,000 property will cost between £300-600.

Mortgage arrangement fees

Depending upon the type of mortgage you are considering you may have to pay an arrangement fee. You should budget for up to £300.

Advice for the investor-letting out property

Importance of having a clear business plan
Letting residential property for profit has become more and more common in the last fifteen years, particularly since the passage of the 1988 Housing Act, which gave potential

landlords more incentive to let, by removing rent controls for property let after 1988 and also changing the tenancy in use to the assured tenancy, a version of which is the assured shorthold, fixed for a minimum period of six months and easily ended after that period.

Added to the passage of the 1988 Act has been the activities of the housing market, which boomed in the eighties and then, predictably, went bust, leaving many in a state of negative equity. The more attractive option for many was to hold on to these properties until the housing market recovered and let them out to cover costs and to achieve a modest return on their investment.

At the time of writing we are experiencing a leveling out (in most areas) of the market after the boom of the last few years. It is also likely that we are heading for a slowing of the property market and a situation where more and more people will rent until prices start to fall. When prices start to fall, again there may be a position of negative equity and owners will let.

In addition to the many who let property out of necessity and who are not "professional landlords" so to speak there are those who have built a business through acquiring properties, mostly through mortgage, and letting them out for a profit. These professional landlords differ as to their expertise, some being very unprofessional in their actual approach, having no idea of Landlord and Tenant law and no idea of the property world and subsequently very little idea of management. Often these people come unstuck and cause grief to others, whether intentionally or otherwise.

The aim of this section is to introduce the landlord, whether potential or already involved in the business, whether professional or merely nursing property through a recession, to the key aspects of the world of residential letting, in the hope that that person becomes more knowledgeable and that profit is maximized whilst management is effective and equitable.

What kind of property is suitable for letting?

Obviously, there are a number of different *markets* when it comes to people who rent. There are those who are less affluent, young and single, in need of a sharing situation, but more likely to require more intensive management than older more mature (perhaps professional) people who can afford a higher rent but require more for their money. The type of property you have, its location, its condition, will very much determine the rent levels that you can charge and the clients that you will attract.

The type of rent that a landlord might expect to achieve will be around ten per cent of the value of the freehold of the property, (or long leasehold in the case of flats). The eventual profit will be determined by the level of any existing mortgage and other outgoings.

If you are renting a flat it could be that it is in a mansion block or other flatted block and the service charge will need to be added to the rent. When letting a property for a profit it is necessary to consider profit after mortgage payments and likely tax bill plus other outgoings such as insurance and agents fees (if any). Of course there are other factors which make the profit achieved less important, that is the capital growth of the property.

The business plan

As a private landlord, a person considering letting a property for profit, or already doing so, it is vital that you are very clear about the following:

- What kind of approach do you intend to take as a landlord? Do you intend to purchase, or do you have, an up market property which you are going to rent out to stable professional tenants who will pay their rent on time and look after the property (hopefully!).

- What are the key factors that affect the value of a property in rental terms? Is the property close to public transport, does it have a garden, what floor is it on and what size are the rooms? Is it secure and in a crime free area. If you are acquiring a property you should set out what it is you are trying to achieve in the longer term, i.e., the type of person you want and match this to the likely residential requirements of that hypothetical person. You can then gain an idea of what type of property you are looking for, in what area, and you can then see whether or not you can afford such a property. If not, you may have to change your plan.

- Do you intend to let to young single people, perhaps students, who will occupy individual rooms, achieving higher returns but causing potentially greater headaches? Are you aware of the headaches? It is vitally important that you understand the ramifications of letting to different client groups and the potential problems in the future.

- Are you clear about the impact on the environment, and to other people that your activities as a landlord may have? For example, do you have a maintenance plan which ensures that not only does your property look nice, and remain well maintained, but also takes into account whether the plan, or lack of it, will have an impact on the rest of the neighborhood? Will the type of tenant you intend to attract affect the rest of those living in the immediate vicinity?

What are the aims and objectives underpinning your business plan? Do you have a business plan or are you operating in an unstructured way? Taking into account the above, it is obviously necessary that you have a clear picture of the business environment that you intend to operate in, the legal and economic framework that governs and regulates the environment.

It is vital that you are very clear about what it is you are trying to achieve. You should either understand the type of property that you already own or have an idea of the property you are trying to acquire to fit what client group. These goals should be very clear in your own mind and based on a long-term projection, underpinned by knowledge of the law and economics of letting property for a profit.

As an exercise you should sit down and map out your business plan, before you go any further. Whether you are an existing property owner, or wish to acquire a property for the purpose of letting, the first objective is to formulate a business plan.

In chapter two we will look more closely at the main considerations when purchasing a property for let

Now you should read the main points from Chapter One overleaf.

Main points from chapter 1

- Give careful thought to all the costs of buying property.

- Banks dealing with buy to let mortgages will normally lend up to 85% of the purchase price of a property. The more that you lend the more that it costs.

- If the house or flat costs over £120,000, stamp duty will be payable.

- You should consider very carefully the need for a full structural survey when buying a property.

- Always Bargain, never offer the asking price.

- There are a number of different markets when it comes to people who rent. The markets are defined mainly be economic factors.

- The type of rent a landlord will expect will vary and the profit will be determined by size of mortgage in relation to rent and also by other outgoings on the property.

- It is vital that a landlord, or prospective landlord, has a business plan that sets out aims and objectives of investment.

- It is vital that you are clear about what you are trying to achieve.

2

LOOKING FOR A PROPERTY

....

Obviously, where you choose to buy your property will be your own decision. However, it may be your first time and you may be at a loss as to where to buy, i.e. rural areas or urban areas, the type and cost of property or whether a house or flat. There are several considerations here. The main consideration if it is a buy to let property is the letting potential and security of your asset, i.e. will it appreciate or will it depreciate.

Area

Buying in a built up area has its advantages and disadvantages. There is usually more demand for property As far as letting is concerned, there are obvious advantages in that there are normally more close communities, because of the sheer density. Local services are closer to hand and there is a greater variety of housing for sale. Transport links are also usually quite good and there are normally plenty of shops.

Disadvantages are less space, less privacy, more local activity, noise and pollution, less street parking, more expensive insurance and different schooling environments to rural environments. The incidence of crime and vandalism and levels of overall stress are higher in built up, more urban areas.

This is not the case with all built up areas. It is up to the buyer to carry out research before making a commitment.

If you are thinking of buying in a rural area, you might want to consider the following: there is more detached housing with land, more space and privacy. There is also cleaner air and insurance premiums can be lower.

Disadvantages can be isolation, loneliness, lower level of services generally, limited choice of local education, therefore the property will be harder to let.

Choosing your property

You should think carefully when considering purchasing a larger property. You may encounter higher costs prior to letting, and also costs that may deter the would be tenant which may include:

- Larger more expensive carpeting
- More furniture. If you are letting your property furnished then you will need to outlay more at the outset
- Larger gardens to tend. Although this may have been one of the attractions, large gardens are time consuming, expensive and hard work.
- Bigger bills
- More decorating
- Higher overall maintenance costs

Purchasing a flat

There are some important points to remember when purchasing a flat. These are common points that are overlooked. For example, if you are buying a flat in a block that is leasehold you will need permission to sublet. This may pose difficulties depending on the freeholder.

Maintenance charge. If you purchase a flat in a block, the costs of maintenance of the flat will be your own. However, the costs of maintaining the common parts will be down to the landlord (usually) paid for by you through a service charge.

There has been an awful lot of trouble with service charges, trouble between landlord and leaseholder. It has to be said that many landlords see service charges as a way of making profit over and above other income, which is usually negligible after sale of a lease.

Many landlords will own the companies that carry out the work and retain the profit made by these companies. They will charge leaseholders excessively for works, which are often not needed. The 1996 Housing Act attempts to strengthen the hand of leaseholders against unscrupulous landlords by making it very difficult indeed for landlords to take legal action for forfeiture (repossession) of lease without first giving the leaseholder a chance to challenge the service charges.

Be very careful if you are considering buying a flat in a block You should establish levels of service charges and look at accounts. Try to elicit information from other leaseholders.

It could be that there is a leaseholders organization, formed to manage their own service charges. This will give you direct control over contracts such as gardening, cleaning, maintenance contacts and cyclical decoration contracts. Better value for money is obtained in this way. In this case, at least you know that the levels will be fair, as no one leaseholder stands to profit.

All of the above should be considered as the profit that you make from letting your property can be greatly diminished by extra costs such as maintenance charges to a freeholder.

Extending your lease

Leasehold Reform Act 1993-as amended by Commonhold and Leasehold Reform Act 2002.

Under this Act, all leaseholders have the right to extend the length of their lease by a term of 90 years. For example, if your lease has 80 years left to run you can extend it to 170 Years. There is a procedure in the above Act for valuation. Leaseholders can collectively also purchase the freehold of the block. There is a procedure for doing this in the Act although it is often time consuming and can be expensive. There are advantages however, particularly when leaseholders are not satisfied with management.

Viewing properties

Before you start house hunting, draw up a list of characteristics you will need from a property, such as the number of bedrooms, size of kitchen, garage and study and garden. Take the estate agents details with you when viewing. Also, take a tape measure with you.

Assess the location of the property. Look at all the aspects and the surroundings. Give some thought as to the impact this will have ability to rent.

Assess the building. Check the facing aspect of the property, i.e., north, south etc. Check the exterior carefully. Earlier, I talked about the need to be very careful when assessing a property. When you have made your mind up, a survey is essential.

Look for a damp proof course - normally about 15cm from the ground. Look for damp inside and out. Items like leaking rainwater pipes should be noted, as they can be a cause of damp. Look carefully at the windows. Are they rotten? Do they need replacing and so on. Look for any cracks. These should most certainly be investigated. A crack can be symptomatic of something worse or it can merely be surface. If you are not in a position to make this judgment then others should make it for you.

Heating is important. If the house or flat has central heating you will need to know when it was last tested. Gas central heating should be tested at least once a year.

All in all you need to remember that you cannot see everything in a house, particularly on the first visit. A great deal may be being concealed from you. In addition, your own knowledge of property may be slim. A second opinion is a must.

Buying a listed building

Buildings of architectural or historical interest are listed by the Secretary of State for National Heritage following consultation with English Heritage, to protect them against inappropriate alteration. In Wales, buildings are listed by the Secretary of State for Wales in consultation with CADW (Heritage Wales). In Scotland, they are listed by the Secretary of State for Scotland, in consultation with Historic Scotland.

If you intend to carry out work to a listed building, you are likely to need listed building consent for any internal or external work, in addition to planning permission. The conservation officer in the local planning department can provide further information.

Buildings in conservation areas

Local authorities can designate areas of special architectural or historical significance. Conservation areas are protected to ensure that their character or interest is retained. Whole towns or villages may be conservation areas or simply one particular street.

Strict regulations are laid down for conservation areas. Protection includes all buildings and all types of trees that are larger than 7cnm across at 1.5m above the ground. There may be limitations for putting up signs, outbuilding or items such as satellite dishes. Any developments in the area usually have to meet strict criteria, such as the use of traditional or local materials.

This also applies to property in national parks, designated Areas of Outstanding natural Beauty and the Norfolk or Suffolk Broads.

Whether or not a property is listed or is deemed to be in a conservation area will show up when your conveyancer carries out the local authority search.

Buying a new house

There are a number of benefits to buying a new house. You have the advantages of being the first owner. There should not be a demand for too much maintenance or DIY jobs, as the building is new.

There will however be a defects period, which usually runs for 6 months for building and 12 months for electrical mechanical. During this period you should expect minor problems, such as cracking of walls, plumbing etc, which will be the responsibility of the builder.

Energy loss will be minimal. A new house today uses 50 per cent less energy than a house built 15 years ago; consider the savings over an older property.

An energy rating indicates how energy efficient a house is. The National House Building Council uses rating scheme based on the National energy services scheme, in which houses are giving a rating between 0 and 10. A house rated 10 will be very energy efficient and have very low running costs for its size.

Security and safety are built in to new houses, smoke alarms are standard and security locks on doors and windows are usually included.

When the house market is slow developers usually offer incentives to buyers, such as cash back, payment of deposit etc.

Building Guarantees

All new houses should be built to certain standards and qualify for one of the building industry guarantees. These building guarantees are normally essential for you to obtain a mortgage and they also make the property attractive to purchasers when you sell. A typical Guarantee is the National House building Council Guarantee (NHBC).

Now read the main points from Chapter Two.

Main points from Chapter Two

- When looking for a house, consider essential points such as area and services.

- Think carefully about costs involved and also work if you are considering buying a larger property.

- When purchasing a flat, consider maintenance charges.

- Before viewing, draw up a list of characteristics you will need from a house or flat.

- There are a number of advantages to buying a new house, such as new construction and minimal energy loss.

3

THE PROCESS OF BUYING A PROPERTY

....

Having considered the costs of acquisition of property, the next step is to find the property you want. This is a long and sometimes dispiriting process. Trudging around estate agents, sorting through mountains of literature, dealing with estate agents details, scouring the papers and walking the streets! However, most of us find the property we want at the end of the day. It is then that we can put in our offer.

Seller's packs

As mentioned in the previous chapter, from June 2007, all people selling a house will be obliged, under the 2004 Housing Act, to provide a seller's pack to potential purchasers. This will consist of, basically, a condition survey, evidence of title and background information about the area and property, such as insurance. There is a significant cost involved in compiling this pack but it is designed to make the process more transparent and quicker over.

Making an offer

You should put your offer in to the estate agent or direct to the seller, depending who you are buying from.

As discussed earlier, your offer should be based on sound judgment, on what the property is worth not on your desire to secure the property at any cost. A survey will help you to arrive at a schedule of works and cost. If you cannot afford to employ a surveyor from a high street firm then you should try to enlist other help.

In addition, you should take a long and careful look at the house yourself, not just a cursory glance. Look at everything and try to get an idea of the likely cost to you of rectifying defects. However, I cannot stress enough the importance of getting a detailed survey.

Eventually, you will be in a position to make an offer for the property. You should base this offer on sound judgment and you should provide a rationalization for your offer, if it is considerably lower than the asking price. You should make it clear that your offer is subject to contract and survey (if you require further examination or wish to carry out a survey after the offer).

Exchange of contracts
Once the buyer and seller are happy with all the details stated in the contract and your conveyancer can confirm that there are no outstanding legal queries, there will be an exchange of contracts. The sale is now legally binding for both parties. You should arrange the necessary insurances, buildings and contents from this moment on, as you are now responsible for the property.

Completing a sale
This is the final day of the sale and normally takes place around ten days after Exchange. Exchange and completion can

take place on the same day if necessary but this is unusual. On day of completion, you are entitled to vacant possession and will receive the keys.

Buying a property in an auction

Property can be purchased in an auction. A small amount are sold in this way. Usually properties sold at auction are either unusual or difficult to put a price on or are repossessions. Auction lists can be obtained from larger estate agents or are advertised in papers. the Estate Gazette, published by the Royal Institute of Chartered Surveyors give details of auctions in each publication. Normally, this magazine is available to subscribers only although it can be ordered through a newsagent.

Preparing for auction

Because the auction is the final step of the sale, you should have any conveyancing carried out and your mortgage arranged. Auctions are a quick way of finding a property if you need to move quite quickly. However, it is likely that your choice of property may be limited and you will need to work on it. Many properties at auction are sub standard, this is why they are there in the first place.

- Ask for the package compiled by the auctioneer. It will include full details of the property and the memorandum of agreement, which is equivalent to the contract.
- View the house
- Organize a conveyancer and instruct him to carry out searches and arrange surveys

- If you like the property, set yourself a price limit to bid to, and arrange a mortgage.

Buying before auction

If the sales details quote "unless previously sold" the seller may be prepared to accept offers before the auction, but he will still accept a fast sale and you will be signing an auction contract. You will need to arrange conveyancing and finance very quickly. If you are buying at the auction itself, you should remember that the fall of the hammer on your bid is equivalent to the exchange of contracts as for a private sale. You have made a legal arrangement and you will be expected to pay 10-15% deposit on the spot with the remainder of the payment within 28 days.

At the auction

If you are doubtful about your own ability then you can appoint a professional to act on your behalf although they will obviously charge for their services.

The seller may be selling subject to a reserve price. If this is the case, it is normally stated in the particulars. The actual figure is not usually disclosed but if the auctioneer states something like "I am going to sell this property today" it is an indication that the reserve price has been reached.

Sale by tender

As an alternative to auction, sale by tender is like a blind auction; you don't know what the other potential buyers are offering. A form of tender is included in the sales details and sometimes sets out the contract details. Always check these details with your conveyancer, because often you cannot pull out after the offer is accepted.

Buyers put their offers in an envelope, sometimes with a 10% deposit. These must be received by the seller's agent at a specified date, at which time the seller will accept one of the offers.

Sale by tender is sometimes used when there have been two or three offers at similar prices.

Now read the Main Points from Chapter Three overleaf.

Main points from Chapter Three

- Make an offer on what you think the property is worth and not the asking price.

- Look over the property you wish to buy very carefully indeed.

- If purchasing jointly, draw up a cohabitation contract.

- If you are buying in an auction take great care.

PART 2

LETTING THE PROPERTY

4

FINDING A TENANT

....

Having examined the whole process underpinning the purchase of a property, from the finances to the location, we will now follow on, logically, and examine the process of letting the property. The following two chapters will cover how and where to find a tenant, the different types of letting and also discuss benefits. In addition, we will look at the nature of the dwelling and what the landlord is expected to provide under the tenancy agreement.

Having laid out your business plan, based on the considerations outlined in chapter one, and given much thought to the purchase of a property to let, it is now necessary to look at the possible sources of the tenant for your property. Remember, the tenant is the key to your future income and profit and also to your own personal peace or otherwise and therefore must be chosen extremely carefully. On the basis of your business plan you will know the type of person that you are prepared to accept because you will have identified what type of management scenario you wish. You will know their position, i.e., whether professional, student, working or on benefits or retired. In order to locate this person you will need to know the various sources available to you.

Letting Agents

There are obvious advantages in using an agent: they are likely to have tenants on their books; they are likely to be experienced and can vet tenants properly before signing a tenancy; they can provide you with a tenancy agreement and they can provide a service after the property is let. However, agent's charge for this service and their fees can vary enormously. It is up to you as a would-be landlord to ensure you understand what it is they are charging and exactly what you are left with after the charges.

Some agencies will offer a guaranteed income for the duration of the contract that you have signed with them, even if a tenant leaves. However, you should be extremely careful here as a number of cases recently against such agencies have revealed that there are unscrupulous operators around.

If you do appoint an agent to manage a property you should agree at the outset, in writing, exactly what constitutes management. Failure to understand the deal between you and the agent can cost you dearly. For example, in a lot of cases, an agent will charge you a fixed fee, sometimes 1 months rental, for finding a tenant, but will then exercise the right that they have given themselves in the initial contract to sign a new agreement and charge another months rent after the tenancy has expired. In this way they will charge you a months rent every six months for doing nothing at all.

Agents will typically look after the following:

- Transfer the utility bills and the council tax into the name of the tenant.

- Paying for repairs, although an agent will only normally do this if rent is being paid directly to them and they can make appropriate deductions.
- Chase rent arrears
- Serve notices of intent to seek possession if the landlord instructs them to do. An agent cannot commence court proceedings except through a solicitor.
- Visit the property at regular intervals check that the tenants are not causing any damage.
- Dealing with neighbor complaints
- Banking rental receipts if the landlord is abroad
- Dealing with housing benefit departments if necessary.

The extent to which agents actually do any or all of the following really depends on the caliber of the agent. It also depends on the type of agreement you have with the agent. Like your initial business plan, you should be very clear about what it is you want from the agent and how much they charge.

Beware! There are many so-called rental agencies, which have sprang up since the property recession and also the advent of "Buy to Let". These agents are not professional, do not know a thing about property management, are shady and should be avoided like the plague. Shop around and seek a reputable agent.

A typical management fee might be 10-15% of the rent, although, as stated, there are many ways of charging and you should be clear about this. It is illegal for agencies to charge tenants for giving out a landlord's name and address. Most agencies will charge the landlord.

Advertisements

The classified advertisement section of local papers is a good place to seek potential tenants, particularly if you wish to avoid agency charges. Local papers are obviously cheaper than the nationals such as the Evening Standard in London or the broadsheets such as the Guardian. The type of newspaper you advertise in will largely reflect what type of customer you are looking for. An advert in the pages of the Times would indicate that you are looking for a well-heeled professional and this would be reflected in the type of property that you have to let.

There are many free ad papers and also you may want to go to student halls of residence or hospitals in order to attract a potential tenant.

When you do advertise, you should indicate clearly the type of property, in what area, what is required, i.e., male or female only, and the rent. You should try and avoid abbreviations as this causes confusion.

The public sector

One other source of income is the local authority or housing association. Quite often, your property will be taken off your hands under a five-year contract and you will receive a rental income paid direct for this period, with agreed increases. However, the local authority or housing association will demand a high standard before taking the property off your hands and quite often the rent achieved will be lower than a comparable market rent, in return for full management and secure income. If you wish to try this avenue then you should contact your local authority or nearest large association.

Company lets

Where the tenant is a company rather than an individual, the tenancy agreement will be similar to an assured shorthold, but will not be bound by the six-month rule (see chapter 7 for details of assured shorthold tenancies). Company lets can be from any length of time, from a week to several years, or as long as you like.

The major difference between contracts and standard Assured shorthold agreements is that the contract will be tailored to individual needs, and the agreement is bound by the provisions of contract law. Company tenancies are bound by the provisions of contract law and not by the 1988 Housing Act. Note: if you are considering letting to a company you must use a letting agent or solicitor. Most companies will insist on it.

The advantages of a landlord letting to a company are:

- A company or embassy has no security of tenure and therefore cannot be a sitting tenant.
- A company cannot seek to reduce the rent by statutory interventions.
- Rental payments are often made quarterly or six monthly in advance.
- The financial status of a company is usually more secure than that of an individual.
- Company tenants often require long term lets to accommodate staff relocating on contracts of between one and five years.

The main disadvantages of company lets are:

- A company tenancy can only be to a bona fide company or embassy, not to a private individual.
- A tenancy to a partnership would not count as a company let and may have some security of tenure.
- If the tenant is a foreign government, the diplomatic status of the occupant must be ascertained, as the courts cannot enforce breaches of contract with somebody who possesses diplomatic immunity.
- A tenancy to a foreign company not registered in the U.K may prove time consuming and costly if it becomes necessary to pursue claims for unpaid rent or damage through foreign courts.

Short lets

Although company lets can be of any length, it is becoming increasingly popular for company's to rent flats from private landlords on short lets.

A short let is any let of less than n six months. But here, it is essential to check the rules with any borough concerned. Some boroughs will not allow lets for less than three months, as they do not want to encourage transient people in the neighborhood.

Generally speaking, short lets are only applicable in large cities where there is a substantial shifting population. Business executives on temporary relocation, actors and others involved in television production or film work, contract workers and visiting academics are examples of people who might require a short let.

From a landlord's point of view, short lets are an excellent idea if you have to vacate your own home for seven or eight months, say, and do not want to leave it empty for that time. Short let tenants provide useful extra income as well as keeping an eye on the place. Or, if you are buying a new property and have not yet sold the old one, it can make good business sense e to let it to a short let tenant.

Short let tenants are, usually, from a landlord's point of view, excellent blue-chip occupants. They are busy professionals, high earners, out all day and used to high standards. As the rent is paid by the company there is no worry for the landlord on this score either.

A major plus of short lets is that they command between 20-50% more rent than the optimum market rent for that type of property. The one downside of short lets is that no agency can guarantee permanent occupancy.

Student lets

Many letting agencies will not consider students and a lot of landlords similarly are not keen. There is the perception that students will not look after a home and tend to live a lifestyle guaranteed to increase the wear and tear on a property. However, if handled correctly, student lets can be profitable. Although students quite often want property for only eight or none months, agencies that deal with students make them sign for a whole year. Rent is guaranteed by confirmation that the student is a genuine student with references from parents, who act as guarantors.

There can be a lot of money made from student lets. However, the tenancy will require more avid policing because of the nature of student lifestyle.

The DSS and housing benefit

Very few letting agencies or landlords will touch DSS or housing benefits tenants. However, as with student lets, there is another side of the coin.

Quite often it is essential for a tenant on HB to have a guarantor, usually a homeowner, before signing a tenancy. Then it is up to the machinations of the benefit system to ensure that the landlord receives rent. The rent is assessed by a benefit officer, with the rent estimated usually at market price. There are rent levels set for each are that the benefit officer will not go above.

A deposit is paid normally and rent is paid direct to the landlord. No other conditions can be accepted by a private landlord. Rent certainly cannot be paid direct to the tenant.

Although tenants on HB have a bad name, due to stereotyping, there are many reasons why a person may be on benefit and probably does not fit the picture of a scrounger who will trash a property. If housing benefit tenancies are manages well, then this can be a useful source of tenant.

Holiday lets

Before the Housing Act 1988 became law, many landlords advertised their properties as holiday lets to bypass the then rules regarding security of tenure. Strictly speaking, a holiday let is a property let for no more than a month to any one tenant. If the same tenant renews for another month then the landlord is breaking the law. Nowadays, holiday lets must be just that-let for a genuine holiday.

If you have a flat or cottage that you wish to let for holiday purposes, whether or not you live in it yourself for part of the year, you are entering into a quite different agreement with the tenant.

Holiday lets are not covered by the Housing Act. The contract is finalized by exchange of letters with the tenant where they place a deposit and the owner confirms the booking. If the let is not for a genuine holiday you may have problems in evicting the tenant, as the whole point of a holiday let is that it is for no more than a fixed period of a month.

Generally speaking, certain services must be provided for the let to be deemed a holiday let. Cleaning services and changes of bed linen are essential. The amount paid by the holiday maker will usual include utilities but would exclude use of the telephone, fax machine etc.

If you have a property that you think is suitable for holiday let or wish to invest in one, there are numerous companies who will take you on to their books. However, standards are high and there are a certain number of criteria to be met, such as safety checks, before they will consider taking you on.

If possible, you should talk to someone with some experience of this type of let before entering into an agreement with an agency. The usual problems may arise, those of ensuring occupancy al year round and the maintenance of your property, which will be higher due to a high turnover.

Bedsits

Bedsitting rooms are usually difficult to let and can cause problems. It is best to leave this area of letting alone. There are numerous regulations to adhere to. Houses in Multiple Occupation regulations are quite strict. The Housing Act 2004 has introduced new tougher regulations for HMO's. If a landlord is letting out property in a block with more than three unrelated dwellings then a licence will be needed from the local authority before lettings can take place. You should contact your Local Authority if you are in this position. There is a problem also of high turnover. Leave this kind of letting to others and concentrate on houses or flats.

Showing the property to the tenant

Once you have found a tenant, the next stage is to make arrangements for viewing the property. It is a good idea to make all appointments on the same day in order to avoid wasting time. If you decide on a likely tenant, it is wise to take up references yourself, if you are not using an agency, who will do this for you. This will normally be a previous landlord's reference and also a bank reference plus a personal reference. Only when these have been received and you have established that the person(s) are safe should you go ahead. Make sure that no keys have been handed over until the cheque has been cleared and you are in receipt of a month's rent and a month's deposit.

Rental guarantees

The landlord is always advised to obtain a guarantor if there is any potential uncertainty as to payment of rent. One example is where the tenant is on benefits. The guarantor will be expected to assume responsibility for the rent if the tenant ceases to pay at any time during the term of the tenancy. There is a sample guarantee form in the appendix to this book.

Be strictly business like. You are letting property for a profit and the tenants are the key to that profit. A mistake at the outset can cost you dearly for a long time to come. See chapter 13 and 15 for further information concerning the start of the tenancy.

In chapter six we will explore the legal framework governing residential lettings.

Now read the main points from Chapter Four.

Main points from chapter four

- The right choice of tenant is crucial as this is the key to the return on your investment.

- You should make sure that you have all the facts about a letting agents terms and conditions before you enter into an agreement.

- The classified advertisement section in the local paper is a good place to seek potential tenants, especially if you wish to manage the property yourself.

- The public sector offers a full management service but often offer a lower rent.

- There are other avenues to explore, such as company lets, short lets, holiday lets and so on. Make sure that you fully understand the various markets and what each entails before entering into an agreement.

- Make sure that, when you have found a tenant, that you take up references and a deposit, and ensure that the tenant is fully aware of all relevant details.

5

WHAT SHOULD BE PROVIDED UNDER THE TENANCY

....

Furniture

A landlords decision whether or not to furnish property will depend on the sort of tenant that he is aiming to find. The actual legal distinction between a furnished property and an unfurnished property has faded into insignificance.

If a landlord does let a property as furnished then the following would be the absolute minimum:

- Seating, such as sofa and armchair

- Cabinet or sideboard

- Kitchen tables and chairs

- Cooker and refrigerator

- Bedroom furniture

Even unfurnished lets, however, are expected to come complete with a basic standard of furniture, particularly carpets and kitchen goods. If the landlord does supply electrical equipment then he or she is able to disclaim any repairing responsibility for it, but this must be mentioned in the tenancy agreement.

Services
Usually, a landlord will only provide services to a tenant if the property is a flat situated in a block or is a house on a private estate. The services will include cyclical painting and maintenance, usually on a three to four year basis (flats) and gardening and cleaning plus repairs to the communal areas, plus communal electricity bills and water rates. These services should be outlined in the agreement and are administered within a strict framework of law, The 1985 Landlord and Tenant Act Section 18-30 as amended by the 1987 LTA.

The landlord has rigid duties imposed within this Act, such as the need to gain estimates before commencing works and also to consult with residents where the cost exceeds £250 per flat. The landlord must give the tenant 28 days notice of works to be carried out and a further 28 days to consider estimates, inviting feedback

Tenants have the right to see audited accounts and invoices relating to work. Service charges, as an extra payment over and above the rent are always contentious and it is an area that Landlords need to be aware of if they are to manage professionally.

Repairs
See chapter on repairing obligations

Insurance
Strictly speaking, there is no duty on either landlord or tenant to insure the property. However, it is highly advisable for the landlord to provide buildings insurance as he/she stands to lose a lot more in the event of fire or other disaster than the tenant.

A landlord letting property for a first time would be well advised to consult his/ her insurance company before letting as there are different criteria to observe when a property is let and not to inform the company could invalidate the policy.

At the end of the tenancy
The tenancy agreement will normally spell out the obligations of the tenant at the end of the term. Essentially, the tenant will have an obligation to:

- have kept the interior clean and tidy and in a good state of repair and decoration

- have not caused any damage

- have replaced anything that they have broken

- replace or pay for the repair of anything that they have damaged

- pay for the laundering of the linen

- pay for any other laundering

- put anything that they have moved or removed back to how it was

Sometimes a tenancy agreement will include for the tenants paying for anything that is soiled at their own expense, although sensible wear and tear is allowed for. The landlord will normally be able to recover any loss from the deposit that the tenant has given on entering the premises. However, sometimes, the tenants will withhold rent for the last month in order to recoup their deposit. It is up to the landlord to negotiate reimbursement for any damage caused, but this should be within reason. There is a remedy, which can be pursued in the Small Claims court if the tenants refuse to pay but this is rarely successful.

Now read the Main points from Chapter Five

Main points from Chapter Five

- A landlord's decision to furnish a property will depend on the sort of tenant he is aiming to find.

- Even unfurnished lets are expected to come complete with a basic standard of furniture.

  - Usually, the landlord will only supply services to a tenant if the flat is in a block or a house on a private estate.

  - If services are provided tenants have a right to audited accounts annually.

PART 3

THE LAW

Tenancies
Quiet enjoyment
Regaining possession
Maintaining a property

6

MANAGING PROPERTY-THE LAW

....

Having examined the processes of purchasing a property and finding a tenant to live in the property and provide the much needed income, we will now look at the whole question of the law that regulates the relationship between landlord and property and landlord and tenant.

Housing professionals exist in all sectors of the economy, private landlords, public landlords, corporate landlords, commercial landlords and so on. Professionals undergo many years of rigorous training in order to gain qualifications. New landlords to the sector are investing for profit and quite often will entrust their property to an agent or will undertake the task themselves. However, it is of the utmost importance that you at least have a basic understanding of the law which will affect you once you have invested in property. The following chapters cover the law generally, the different types of tenancy, going to court and repairing obligations.

Explaining the law

As a landlord or potential landlord it is very important to understand the rights and obligations of both yourself and your tenant, exactly what can and what cannot be done once the tenancy agreement has been signed and the tenant has moved into the property.

Some landlords think they can do exactly as they please, because the property belongs to them. Some tenants do not know any differently and therefore the landlord can, and often does, get away with breaking the law. However, if you are about to embark upon a career as a budding landlord, letting property, then it is important that you have a grasp on the key principles of the law.

In order to fully understand the law we should begin by looking at the main types of relationship between people and their homes.

The freehold and the lease

In law, there are two main types of ownership and occupation of property. These are: freehold and leasehold. These arrangements are very old indeed.

Freehold

If a person owns their property outright (usually with a mortgage) then they are a freeholder.

The only claims to ownership over and above their own might be those of the building society or the bank, which lent them the money to buy the place. They will re-possess the property if the mortgage payments are not kept up with.

In certain situations though, the local authority (council) for an area can affect a person's right to do what they please with their home even if they are a freeholder. This will occur when planning powers are exercised, for example, in order to prevent the carrying out of alterations without consent.

The local authority for your area has many powers and we will be referring to these regularly in each Chapter of this Guide.

Leasehold

If a person lives in a property owned by someone else and has a written agreement allowing them to occupy the flat or house for a period of time i.e., giving them permission to live in that property, then they will, in the main, have a lease and either be a leaseholder or a tenant of a landlord.

The main principle of a lease is that a person has been given permission by someone else to live in his or her property for a period of time. The person giving permission could be either the freeholder or another leaseholder.

The tenancy agreement is one type of lease. If you have issued a tenancy agreement then you will have given permission to a person live in your property for a period of time.

The position of the tenant

The tenant will usually have an agreement for a shorter period of time than the typical leaseholder. Whereas the leaseholder will, for example, have an agreement for ninety-nine years, the tenant will have an agreement, which either runs from week to week or month to month (periodic tenancy) or is for a fixed term, for example, one year. These arrangements are the most common types of agreement between the private landlord and tenant.

The agreement itself will state whether it is a fixed term or periodic tenancy. If an agreement has not been issued it will be assumed to be a periodic tenancy.

Both periodic and fixed term tenants will usually pay a sum of rent regularly to a landlord in return for permission to live in the property (more about rent and service charges later)

The tenancy agreement

The tenancy agreement is the usual arrangement under which one person will live in a property owned by another. Before a tenant moves into a property he/she will have to sign a tenancy agreement drawn up by a landlord or landlord's agent. *A tenancy agreement is a contract between landlord and tenant.*

It is important to realize that when you sign a tenancy agreement, you have signed a contract with another person, which governs the way in which they will live in their property.

The contract

Typically, any tenancy agreement will show the name and address of the landlord and will state the names of the tenant(s). The type of tenancy agreement that is signed should be clearly indicated. This could be, for example, a Rent Act protected tenancy, an assured tenancy or an assured shorthold tenancy. In the main, the agreement will be an assured shorthold.

The date the tenancy began and the duration (fixed term or periodic) plus the amount of rent payable should be clearly shown, along with who is responsible for any other charges, such as water rates, council tax etc, and a description of the property you are renting out.

In addition to the rent that must be paid there should be a clear indication of when a rent increase can be expected. This information is sometimes shown in other conditions of tenancy, which should be given to the tenant when they move into their home. The conditions of tenancy will set out landlords and tenants rights and obligations.

If services are provided, i.e., if a service charge is payable, this should be indicated in the agreement. The tenancy agreement should indicate clearly the address to which notices on the landlord can be served by the tenant, for example, because of repair problems or notice of leaving the property. The landlord has a legal requirement to indicate this.

The tenancy agreement will either be a basic document with the above information or will be more comprehensive. Either way, there will be a section beginning "the tenant agrees." Here the tenant will agree to move into the property, pay rent, use the property as an only home, not cause a nuisance to others, take responsibility for certain internal repairs, not sublet the property, i.e., create another tenancy, and various other things depending on the property.

There should also be another section "the landlord agrees". Here, the landlord is contracting with the tenant to allow quiet enjoyment of the property. The landlord's repairing responsibilities are also usually outlined.

Finally, there should be a section entitled "ending the tenancy" which will outline the ways in which landlord and tenant can end the agreement. It is in this section that the landlord should make reference to the "grounds for possession". Grounds for possession are circumstances where the landlord will apply to court for possession of his/her property. Some of these grounds relate to what is in the tenancy, i.e., the responsibility to pay rent and to not cause a nuisance.

Other grounds do not relate to the contents of the tenancy directly, but more to the law governing that particular tenancy. The grounds for possession are very important, as they are used in any court case brought against the tenant.

Unfortunately, they are not always indicated in the tenancy agreement. As they are so important they are summarized later on in this chapter.

It must be said at this point that many residential tenancies are very light on landlord's responsibilities. Repairing responsibilities, and responsibilities relating to rental payment, are landlords obligations under law. This book deals with these, and other areas. However, many landlords will seek to use only the most basic document in order to conceal legal obligations.

The public sector tenancy (local authority or housing association), for example, is usually very clear and very comprehensive about the rights and obligations of landlord and tenant. Unfortunately, the private landlord often does not employ the same energy when it comes to educating and informing the tenant. This is one of the main reasons for this book. It is essential that those who intend to let property for profit are able to manage professionally and set high standards as a private landlord. This is because the sector has been beset by rogues in the past.

Appendix 1 shows what a typical residential tenancy agreement should look like.

The responsibility to provide a tenant with a rent book

If the tenant is a weekly periodic tenant the landlord must provide him/her with a rent book and commits a criminal offence if he/she does not do so. This is outlined in the Landlord and Tenant Act 1985 sections 4 - 7. Under this Act any tenant can ask in writing the name and address of the landlord. The landlord must reply within twenty-one days of asking.

As most tenancies nowadays are fixed term assured shortholds then it is not strictly necessary to provide a tenant with a rent book. However, for the purposes of business efficiency, and your own records, it is always useful to issue a rent book to tenants and sign it each time rent is collected or a standing order is paid.

Overcrowding

It is important to understand, when signing a tenancy agreement, that it is not permitted to allow the premises to become overcrowded, i.e., to allow more people than was originally intended, (which is outlined in the agreement) to live in the property! If a tenant does then the landlord can take action to evict.

Different types of tenancy agreement

The protected tenancy - the meaning of the term

As a basic guide, if a person is a private tenant and signed their current agreement with a landlord before 15th January 1989 then they will, in most cases, be a protected tenant with all the rights relating to protection of tenure, which are considerable. Protection is provided under the 1977 Rent Act.

In practice, there are not many protected tenancies left and the investor will usually be managing an assured shorthold tenancy.

The assured shorthold tenancy - what it means

If the tenant entered into an agreement with a landlord after 15th January 1989 then they will, in most cases, be an assured tenant. We will discuss assured tenancies in more depth in chapter seven. In brief, there are various types of assured tenancy. The assured shothold is usually a fixed term version of the assured tenancy and enables the landlord to recover their property after six months and to vary the rent after this time.

At this point it is important to understand that the main difference between the two types of tenancy, protected and assured, is that the tenant has less rights as a tenant under the assured tenancy. For example, they will not be entitled, as is a protected tenant, to a fair rent set by a Rent Officer.

Other types of agreement

In addition to the above tenancy agreements, there are other types of agreement sometimes used in privately rented property. One of these is the company let, as we discussed in the last chapter, and another is the license agreement. The person signing such an agreement is called a licensee.

Licenses will only apply in special circumstances where the licensee cannot be given sole occupation of his home and therefore can only stay for a short period with minimum rights. It is not the intention to pursue licensees further in this book.

The squatter (trespasser)

In addition to the tenant and licensee, there is one other type of occupation of property, which needs mentioning. This is squatting. It is useful for the would-be landlord to have a basic understanding of this are of occupation.

The squatter is usually someone who has gained entry to a vacant property, either a house or a flat, without permission.

Although the squatter, a trespasser, has the protection of the law and cannot be evicted without a court order, if he or she is to be given the protection of the law, the squatted property must have been empty in the first place.

On gaining entry to a property, the squatter will normally put up a notice claiming squatter's rights, which means that they are identifying themselves as a person or group having legal protection until a court order is obtained to evict them. Even if no notice is visible, the squatter has protection and it is an offence to attempt to remove them forcibly.

The squatter has protection from eviction under the Protection from Eviction Act 1977 and is also protected from violence or harassment by the Criminal Law Act of 1977.

The trespasser who has entered an occupied property without permission has fewer rights. Usually, the police will either arrest or escort a trespasser off the premises. There is no protection from eviction. However, there is protection from violence and intimidation under the Criminal Law Act of 1977.

Now read the main Points from Chapter Six

Main Points from Chapter Six

- **Private Tenant**. A tenant of a landlord who is not a public landlord, public landlord being for example a local authority or housing association. The most common private tenancy relationship is between two individuals or between an individual and a company.

- **Leasehold and freehold**. These are the two main types of ownership of land and occupation of property. A freeholder will own the property outright (usually with a mortgage). A leaseholder has the right to live there for a period of time.

- **Tenancy agreement**. The tenancy agreement is one form of lease. It is a contract between the landlord and tenant for the occupation of property. The tenancy agreement is either for a specific length (e.g., six months) of time or from week to week or month to month. The agreement will govern the length of notice given by the landlord or tenant when requiring the property back, or, in the case of the tenant, leaving the property.

- **Rent book**. If a tenancy is a weekly periodic tenancy, then a landlord must provide a tenant with a rent book.

- **Overcrowding**. A tenant must not allow his/her home to become overcrowded. A landlord can take a tenant to court and can evict in this case.

- **The assured tenant**. This is the usual type of tenancy agreement entered into after 15th January 1989, which is regulated by the 1988 Housing Act. In Chapter 7 we discuss this type of agreement.
- **The license and the licensee**. This is one type of agreement between landlord and tenant, which gives the occupier fewer rights than a protected tenant. More about the license in Chapter Two.

- **The squatter (trespasser)**. The squatter is someone who has entered a vacant property without permission and set up home there. The squatter can be evicted only with a court order. However, someone who has entered an occupied property, has no protection at all and can be removed immediately by the police.

7

ASSURED, ASSURED SHORTHOLD AND JOINT TENANTS

....

The assured tenant

As we discussed in Chapter seven, all tenancies, with the exceptions detailed, entered into after 15th January 1989, are known as assured tenancies. *An assured shorthold tenancy, which is the most common form of tenancy used by the landlord nowadays, is one type of assured tenancy, and is for a fixed term of six months minimum and can be brought to an end with two months notice by serving a section 21 (of the Housing Act 1988) notice.*

Assured tenancies are governed by the 1988 Housing Act, as amended by the 1996 Housing Act. It is to these Acts, or outlines of the Acts that the landlord must refer when intending to sign a tenancy and let a residential property.

For a tenancy to be assured, three conditions must be fulfilled:

1. The premises must be a dwelling house. This basically means any premises, which can be lived in. Business premises will normally fall outside this interpretation.
2. There must exist a particular relationship between landlord and tenant. In other words there must exist a tenancy agreement. For example, a licence to occupy, as in the case

of students, or accommodation occupied as a result of work, cannot be seen as a tenancy. Following on from this, the accommodation must be let as a single unit. The tenant, who must be an individual, must normally be able to sleep, cook and eat in the accommodation. Sharing of
bathroom facilities will not prevent a tenancy being an assured tenancy but shared cooking or other facilities, such as a living room, will.

3. The third requirement for an assured tenancy is that the tenant must occupy the dwelling as his or her only or principal home. In situations involving joint tenants at least one of them must occupy.

Tenancies that are not assured

A tenancy agreement will not be assured if one of the following conditions applies:

-The tenancy or the contract was entered into before 15th January 1989;

-If no rent is payable or if only a low rent amounting to less than two thirds of the present ratable value of the property is payable;

-If the premises are let for business purposes or for mixed residential and business purposes;

-If part of the dwelling house is licensed for the sale of liquor for consumption on the premises. This does not include the publican who lets out a flat;

-If the dwelling house is let with more than two acres of agricultural land;

-If the dwelling house is part of an agricultural holding and is occupied in relation to carrying out work on the holding;

-If the premises are let by a specified institution to students, i.e., halls of residence;

-If the premises are let for the purpose of a holiday;

-Where there is a resident landlord, e.g., in the case where the landlord has let one of his rooms but continues to live in the house;

-If the landlord is the Crown (the monarchy) or a government department. Certain lettings by the Crown are capable of being assured, such as some lettings by the Crown Estate Commissioners;

-If the landlord is a local authority, a fully mutual housing association (this is where you have to be a shareholder to be a tenant) a newly created Housing Action Trust or any similar body listed in the 1988 Housing Act.

-If the letting is transitional such as a tenancy continuing in its original form until phased out, such as:

-A protected tenancy under the 1977 Rent Act;

-Secure tenancy granted before 1st January 1989, e.g., from a local authority or housing association. These tenancies are governed by the 1985 Housing Act).

The Assured Shorthold tenancy

The assured shorthold tenancy as we have seen, is the most common form of tenancy used in the private sector. The main principle of the assured shorthold tenancy is that it is issued for a period of six months minimum and can be brought to an end by the landlord serving two months notice on the tenant. At the end of the six-month period the tenant, if given two months prior notice, by the landlord serving a section 21 notice (see appendix) must leave.

Any property let on an assured tenancy can be let on an assured shorthold, providing the following conditions are met:

- The tenancy must be for a fixed term of not less than six months.
- The agreement cannot contain powers, which enable the landlord to end the tenancy before six months. This does not include the right of the landlord to enforce the grounds for possession, which will be approximately the same as those for the assured tenancy (see below).
- A notice requiring possession at the end of the term is usually served two months before that date.
- A notice must be served before any rent increase giving one months clear notice and providing details of the rent increase.

Getting possession of your property before the end of the tenancy

If the landlord wishes to get possession of his/her property, in this case before the expiry of the contractual term, the landlord has to gain a court order. A notice of seeking possession must be served, giving fourteen days notice and following similar grounds of possession as an assured tenancy (see below).

The landlord cannot simply tell a tenant to leave before the end of the agreed term.

A copy of a notice of seeking possession for an assured (shorthold) tenancy is shown in the Appendix.

Tenancy running on after fixed term

An assured shorthold tenancy will become periodic (will run from week to week) when the initial term of six months has elapsed and the landlord has not brought the tenancy to an end.

If the tenancy runs on after the end of the fixed term then the landlord can regain possession by giving the required two months notice, as mentioned above.

At the end of the term for which the assured shorthold tenancy has been granted, the landlord has an automatic right to possession.

Evicting assured shorthold tenants

As discussed, it is possible to gain possession of a property before the end of the fixed term if the tenancy has been seriously breached. Assured shorthold tenants, can be evicted only on certain grounds some discretionary, some mandatory (see below).

In order for the landlord of an assured shorthold tenant to regain possession of the property, using grounds for possession such as non-payment of rent, a notice of seeking possession (of property) must be served, giving fourteen days notice of expiry and stating the ground for possession.

Following the fourteen days a court order must be obtained. Although gaining a court order is not complicated, a solicitor will usually be used. Court costs can be awarded against the tenant.

Security of tenure: The ways in which a tenant can lose their home as an assured (shorthold) tenant

There are a number of circumstances called grounds (mandatory and discretionary) whereby A landlord can start a court action to evict a tenant.

The following are the *mandatory* grounds (where the judge must give the landlord possession) and *discretionary* grounds (where the judge does not have to give the landlord possession) on which a court can order possession if the home is subject to an assured tenancy.

The mandatory grounds for possession

There are eight mandatory grounds for possession, which, if proved, leave the court with no choice but to make an order for possession. It is very important that you understand these.

Ground One is used where the landlord has served a notice, no later than at the beginning of the tenancy, warning the tenant that this ground may be used against him/her. This ground is used where the landlord wishes to recover the property as his or her principal (first and only) home or the spouse's (wife's or husbands) principal home. *The ground is not available to a person who bought the premises for gain (profit) whilst they were occupied.*

Ground Two is available where the property is subject to a

74

mortgage and if the landlord does not pay the mortgage, could lose the home.

Grounds Three and Four relate to holiday lettings.

Ground Five is a special one, applicable to ministers of religion.

Ground Six relates to the demolition or reconstruction of the property.

Ground Seven applies if a tenant dies and in his will leaves the tenancy to someone else: but the landlord must start proceedings against the new tenant within a year of the death if he wants to evict the new tenant.

Ground Eight concerns rent arrears. This ground applies if, both at the date of the serving of the notice seeking possession and at the date of the hearing of the action, the rent is at least 8 weeks in arrears or two months in arrears. This is the main ground used by landlords when rent is not being paid.

The landlord should understand that in order to get a court order for possession of property for rent arrears then, because of the short-term nature of the Assured shorthold, time is of the essence. If the tenancy is into the third month, it may be easier to wait and serve a two-month notice of termination and get a court order against the occupants separately.

One of the advantages of a court order is that you will have details of the tenant's employers and can get an attachment of earnings against the tenant.

The discretionary grounds for possession of a property

As we have seen, the discretionary grounds for possession are those in relation to which the court has some powers over whether or not the landlord can evict. In other words, the final decision is left to the judge. Often the judge will prefer to grant a suspended order first, unless the circumstances are dramatic.

Ground Nine applies when suitable alternative accommodation is available or will be when the possession order takes effect. As we have seen, if the landlord wishes to obtain possession of his or her property in order to use it for other purposes then suitable alternative accommodation has to be provided.

Ground Ten deals with rent arrears as does ground eleven. These grounds are distinct from the mandatory grounds, as there does not have to be a fixed arrear in terms of time scale, e.g., 8 weeks. The judge, therefore, has some choice as to whether or not to evict. In practice, this ground will not be relevant to managers of assured shorthold tenancies.

Ground Twelve concerns any broken obligation of the tenancy. As we have seen with the protected tenancy, there are a number of conditions of the tenancy agreement, such as the requirement not to racially or sexually harass a neighbor. Ground Twelve will be used if these conditions are broken.

Ground Thirteen deals with the deterioration of the dwelling as a result of a tenant's neglect. This is connected with the structure of the property and is the same as for a protected tenancy. It puts the responsibility on the tenant to look after the premises.

Ground Fourteen concerns nuisance, annoyance and illegal or immoral use. This is where a tenant or anyone connected with the tenant has caused a nuisance to neighbors.

Ground 14A this ground deals with domestic violence.

Ground Fifteen concerns the condition of the furniture and tenants neglect. As Ground thirteen puts some responsibility on the tenant to look after the structure of the building so Ground Fifteen makes the tenant responsible for the furniture and fittings.

The description of the grounds above is intended as a guide only. For a fuller description please refer to the 1988 Housing Act, section 7, Schedule two,) as amended by the 1996 Housing Act) which is available at reference libraries.

As we have discussed, it is usual for the landlord of an assured tenancy to serve a notice requiring possession on the tenant giving two months notice. It is unusual for a landlord to take an assured tenant to court on one of the grounds for possession. However, these circumstances do arise, where a tenant has breached the tenancy very early on and the landlord cannot wait for the fixed term to expire.

Fast track possession

In November 1993, following changes to the County Court Rules, a facility was introduced which enables landlords of tenants with assured shorthold tenancies to apply for possession of their property without the usual time delay involved in waiting for a court date and attendance at court. This is known as "fast track possession" It cannot be used for rent arrears or other grounds. It is used to gain possession of a property when the fixed term of six months or more has come to an end, a valid section 21 notice has been served and the tenant will not move.

Raising rent

If the landlord wishes to raise rent, at least one month's minimum notice must be given. The rent cannot be raised more than once for the same tenant in one year. Tenants have the right to challenge a rent increase if they think it is unfair by referring the rent to a Rent Assessment Committee. The committee will prevent the landlord from raising the rent above the ordinary market rent for that type of property.

Joint tenancies: the position of two or more people who have a tenancy agreement for one property

Although it is the normal state of affairs for a tenancy agreement to be granted to one person, this is not always the case.

A tenancy can also be granted to two or more people and is then known as a *joint tenancy*. The position of joint tenants is exactly the same as that of single tenants. In other words, there is still one tenancy even though it is shared.

Each tenant is responsible for paying the rent and observing the terms and conditions of the tenancy agreement. No one joint tenant can prevent another joint tenant's access to the premises.

If one of the joint tenants dies then his or her interest will automatically pass to the remaining joint tenants. A joint tenant cannot dispose of his or her interest in a will.

If one joint tenant, however, serves a notice to quit (notice to leave the property) on another joint tenant(s) then the tenancy will come to an end and the landlord can apply to court for a possession order, if the remaining tenant does not leave.

The position of a wife or husband in relation to joint tenancies is rather more complex because the married person has more rights when it comes to the home than the single person.

Remember: the position of a tenant who has signed a joint tenancy agreement is exactly the same as that of the single tenant. If one person leaves, the other(s) have the responsibilities of the tenancy. If one person leaves without paying his share of the rent then the other tenants will have to pay instead.

Now read the Main Points from Chapter Seven

Main points from Chapter 7

- **Assured tenancies**. All tenancies signed after 15th January 1989, with a few exceptions, are assured tenancies. The assured shorthold tenancy is one type of assured tenancy and is the one most frequently used by private landlords.

- **Protection**. Assured tenancies are not protected by the 1977 Rent Act and do not have a right to a fair rent.

- **Security**. Assured tenants can only be evicted on certain grounds for possession, after being given a minimum of fourteen days notice and taken to court.

- **Rents**. Assured rents cannot be raised more than once in a one-year period. They can, however, be raised when a fixed term assured shorthold has ended. This may be after six months.

- **Fixed term**. An assured shorthold tenancy is granted for a minimum period of six months. Two months notice has to be given before ending the tenancy. The notice can be served when granting the tenancy bringing it to an end on the last day of the six months. After the six months has elapsed, two months notice can be given anytime. The tenancy can be allowed to run on, it becomes an assured shorthold periodic tenancy, as opposed to fixed term.

- Joint tenants. A tenancy granted to two or more people is a joint tenancy. The position of joint tenants is exactly the same as that of a single tenant.

- Ending the tenancy. In order to end the tenancy, one of the joint tenants must serve a notice to quit on the other tenant(s).

8

THE RIGHT TO QUIET ENJOYMENT OF A HOME

....

Earlier, we saw that when a tenancy agreement is signed, the landlord is contracting to give quiet enjoyment of the tenants home. This means that they have the right to live peacefully in the home without harassment.

The landlord is obliged not to do anything that will disturb the right to the quiet enjoyment of the home. The most serious breach of this right would be for the landlord to wrongfully evict a tenant.

Eviction: what can be done against unlawful harassment and eviction

It is a criminal offence for a landlord unlawfully to evict a residential occupier (whether or not a tenant!). The occupier has protection under the Protection from Eviction Act 1977 section 1(2).

If the tenant or occupier is unlawfully evicted his/her first course should be to seek an injunction compelling the landlord to readmit him/her to the premises.

It is an unfortunate fact but many landlords will attempt to evict tenants forcefully. In doing so they break the law.

However, the landlord may, on termination of the tenancy

recover possession without a court order if the agreement was entered into after 15th January 1989 and it falls into one of the following six situations:

-The occupier shares any accommodation with the landlord and the landlord occupies the premises as his or her only or principal home.

-The occupier shares any of the accommodation with a member of the landlords family, that person occupies the premises as their only or principal home, and the landlord occupies as his or her only or principal home premises in the same building.

-The tenancy or licence was granted temporarily to an occupier who entered the premises as a trespasser.

-The tenancy or licence gives the right to occupy for the purposes of a holiday.

-The tenancy or licence is rent-free.

-The licence relates to occupation of a hostel.

There is also a section in the 1977 Protection from Eviction Act which provides a defense for otherwise unlawful eviction and that is that the landlord may repossess if it is thought that the tenant no longer lives on the premises. It is important to note that, in order for such action to be seen as a crime under the 1977 Protection from Eviction Act, the intention of the landlord to evict must be proved.

However, there is another offence, namely harassment,

which also needs to be proved. Even if the landlord is not guilty of permanently depriving a tenant of their home he/she could be guilty of harassment.

Such actions as cutting off services, deliberately allowing the premises to fall into a state of disrepair, or even forcing unwanted sexual attentions, all constitute harassment and a breach of the right to *quiet enjoyment*.

The 1977 Protection from Eviction Act also prohibits the use of violence to gain entry to premises. Even in situations where the landlord has the right to gain entry without a court order it is an offence to use violence. *If entry to the premises is opposed then the landlord should gain a court order.*

What can be done against unlawful evictions?

There are two main remedies for unlawful eviction: damages and, as stated above, an injunction.

The injunction

An injunction is an order from the court requiring a person to do, or not do, something. In the case of eviction the court can grant an injunction requiring the landlord to allow a tenant back into occupation of the premises. In the case of harassment an order can be made preventing the landlord from harassing the tenant.

Failure to comply with an injunction is contempt of court and can result in a fine or imprisonment.

Damages

In some cases the tenant can press for *financial compensation* following unlawful eviction. Financial compensation may have to be paid in cases where financial loss has occurred or in cases where personal hardship alone has occurred.

The tenant can also press for *special damages,* which means that the tenant may recover the definable out-of-pocket expenses. These could be expenses arising as a result of having to stay in a hotel because of the eviction. Receipts must be kept in that case. There are also *general damages*, which can be awarded in compensation for stress, suffering and inconvenience.

A tenant may also seek *exemplary damages* where it can be proved that the landlord has disregarded the law deliberately with the intention of making a profit out of the displacement of the tenant.

Now read the Main Points from Chapter Twelve.

Main points from Chapter Eight

- **Quiet enjoyment**. A tenant has the right to quiet enjoyment of his/her home.

- **Eviction**. It is a criminal offence to unlawfully evict a tenant from his or her home.

- **Use of force**. There are certain circumstances in which the landlord can recover possession without a court order but he/she cannot use force to evict a tenant.

- **Tenants rights**. If a tenant is unlawfully evicted, he/she can seek an injunction to force the landlord to let them back into their home. They can also seek damages for harassment and inconvenience.

9

REGAINING POSSESSION OF A PROPERTY

....

There may come a time when you need to go to court to regain possession of your property. This will usually arise when the contract has been breached by the tenant, for non-payment of rent or for some other breach such as nuisance or harassment. As we have seen, a tenancy can be brought to an end in a court on one of the grounds for possession. However, as the tenancy will usually be an assured shorthold then it is necessary to consider whether you are in a position to give two months notice and withhold the deposit, as opposed to going to court.

If you decide, for whatever reason, to go to court, then any move to regain your property for breach of agreement will commence in the county court in the area in which the property is. The first steps in ending the tenancy will necessitate the serving of a notice of seeking possession using one of the Grounds for Possession detailed earlier in the book. If the tenancy is protected then 28 days must be given, the notice must be in prescribed form and served on the tenant personally (preferably).

If the tenancy is assured shorthold, which is more often the case now, then 14 days notice of seeking possession can be used. In all cases the ground to be relied upon must be clearly outlined in the notice. If the case is more complex, then this will entail a particulars of claim being prepared, usually by a solicitor, as opposed to a standard possession form.

A fee is paid when sending the particulars to court, which is currently £120. The standard form which the landlord uses for routine rent arrears cases is called the N119 (see appendix) and the accompanying summons is called the N5. Both of these forms can be obtained from the court. When completed, the forms should be sent in duplicate to the county court and a copy retained for you.

The court will send a copy of the Particulars of claim and the summons to the tenant. They will send you a "Plaint note" which gives you a case number and court date to appear, known as the return date.

On the return date, you should arrive at court at least 15 minutes early. You can represent yourself in simple cases but are advised to use a solicitor for more contentious cases.

When it is your turn to present the case, you should have your file in order, a copy of all relevant notices served and a current rent arrears figure or a copy of the particulars for other cases. If it is simple rent arrears then quite often the judge will guide you through. However, the following are the steps to observe:

-State your name and address
-Tenants name and address
-Start date of tenancy
-Current rent and arrears
-Date notice served-a copy should be produced for the judge
-Circumstances of tenant (financial and other) this is where you make your case
-Copy of order wanted

If the tenant is present then they will have a chance to defend themselves.

A number of orders are available. However, if you have gone to court on the mandatory ground eight then if the fact is proved then you will get possession immediately. If not, then the judge can grant an order, suspended whilst the tenant finds time to pay.

In a lot of cases, it is more expedient for a landlord to serve notice-requiring possession, if the tenancy has reached the end of the period, and then wait two months before the property is regained. This saves the cost and time of going to court particularly if the ground is one of nuisance or other, which will involve solicitors.

In many cases, if you are contemplating going to court and have never been before and do not know the procedure then it is best to use a solicitor to guide the case through. Costs can be recovered from the tenant, although this depends on the tenant's means.

If you regain possession of your property midway through the contract term then you will have to complete the possession process by use of bailiff, a fee of £120 and another form, Warrant for Possession of Land used.

If you have reached the end of the contractual term and wish to recover your property then a "fast track" procedure is available which entails gaining an order for possession and bailiff's order by post. This can be used in cases with the exception of rent arrears.

Now read the Main points from Chapter Nine

Main points from Chapter Nine

- One of the unpleasant sides of being a landlord is that you may have to go to court to regain possession of a property.

- Any move to regain possession of your property will commence in the local county court where the property is. Fourteen days service of notice is needed and a fee is payable to the court. It is usually best to employ a solicitor to take this action.

10

REPAIRING OBLIGATIONS

....

Repairs and improvements generally: the landlord and tenants obligations

Repairs are essential works to keep the property in good order. Improvements are alterations to the property, e.g. the installation of a shower.

As we have seen, most tenancies are periodic, i.e. week-to-week or month-to-month. If a tenancy falls into this category, or is a fixed-term tenancy for less than seven years, and began after October1961, then a landlord is legally responsible for most major repairs to the flat or house.

If a tenancy began after 15th January 1989 then, in addition to the above responsibility, the landlord is also responsible for repairs to common parts and service fittings.

The area of law dealing with the landlord and tenants repairing obligations is the 1985 Landlord and Tenant Act, section 11.

This section of the Act is known as a covenant and cannot be excluded by informal agreement between landlord and tenant. In other words the landlord is legally responsible whether he or she likes it or not. Parties to a tenancy, however, may make an application to a court mutually to vary or exclude this section.

An example of repairs a landlord is responsible for:
-Leaking roofs and guttering;
-Rotting windows;
-Rising damp;
-Damp walls;
-Faulty electrical wiring;
-Dangerous ceilings and staircases;
-Faulty gas and water pipes;
-Broken water heaters and boilers;
-Broken lavatories, sinks or baths.

In shared housing the landlord must see that shared halls, stairways, kitchens and bathrooms are maintained and kept clean and lit.

Normally, tenants are responsible only for minor repairs, e.g., broken door handles, cupboard doors, etc. Tenants will also be responsible for decorations unless they have been damaged as a result of the landlord's failure to do repair.

A landlord will be responsible for repairs only if the repair has been reported. It is therefore important to report repairs in writing and keep a copy. If the repair is not carried out then action can be taken. Damages can also be claimed.

Compensation can be claimed, with the appropriate amount being the reduction in the value of the premises to the tenant caused by the landlord's failure to repair. If the tenant carries out the repairs then the amount expended will represent the decrease in value.

The tenant does not have the right to withhold rent because of a breach of repairing covenant by the landlord. However, depending on the repair, the landlord will not have a very strong case in court if rent is withheld.

REPORTING REPAIRS TO LANDLORDS

The tenant has to tell the landlord or the person collecting the rent straight away when a repair needs doing. It is advisable that it is in writing, listing the repairs that need to be done.

Once a tenant has reported a repair the landlord must do it within a reasonable period of time. What is reasonable will depend on the nature of the repair. If certain emergency work needs to be done by the council, such as leaking guttering or drains a notice can be served ordering the landlord to do the work within a short time. In exceptional cases if a home cannot be made habitable at reasonable cost the council may declare that the house must no longer be used, in which case the council has a legal duty to re-house a tenant.

If after the council has served notice the landlord still does not do the work, the council can send in its own builder or, in some cases take the landlord to court. A tenant must allow a landlord access to do repairs. The landlord has to give twenty four hours notice of wishing to gain access.

The tenants rights whilst repairs are being carried out

The landlord must ensure that the repairs are done in an orderly and efficient way with minimum inconvenience to the tenant If the works are disruptive or if property or decorations are damaged the tenant can apply to the court for compensation or, if necessary, for an order to make the landlord behave reasonably.

If the landlord genuinely needs the house empty to do the work he/she can ask the tenant to vacate it and can if necessary get a court order against the tenant.

A *written agreement* should be drawn up making it clear that the tenant can move back in when the repairs are completed and stating what the arrangements for fuel charges and rent are.

If a person is an *assured* tenant the landlord could get a court order to make that person give up the home permanently if there is work to be done with him/her in occupation in occupation.

Can the landlord put the rent up after doing repairs?

If there is a service charge for maintenance, the landlord may be able to pass on the cost of the work(s).

Tenants rights to make improvements to a property

Unlike carrying out repairs the tenant will not normally have the right to insist that the landlord make actual alterations to the home. However, a tenant needs the following amenities and the law states that you should have them:

-Bath or shower;

-Wash hand basin;

-Hot and cold water at each bath, basin or shower;

-An indoor toilet.

If these amenities do not exist then the tenant can contact the council's Environmental Health Officer. An improvement notice can be served on the landlord ordering him to put the amenity in.

Disabled tenants

If a tenant is disabled he/she may need special items of equipment in the accommodation. The local authority may help in providing and, occasionally, paying for these. The tenant will need to obtain the permission of the landlord. If you require more information then contact the social services department locally.

Shared housing. The position of tenants in shared houses (Houses in Multiple Occupation)

The law lays down special standards for shared housing (houses in multiple-occupation). These are usually houses of more three storeys with five or more occupants living in two or more households. Local authorities have special powers to deal with bad conditions when they occur. The legal regulations for houses in multiple-occupation are set out in the Housing (Management of Houses in Multiple Occupation) Regulations 1990 and also the Housing Act 1996, as amended by the Housing Act 2005. The 2005 Act introduced a new licensing scheme for landlords who manage house in multi-occupation.

The manager of a house in multiple-occupation has responsibilities under the management regulations to carry out repair, maintenance and cleaning work and also safety work necessary to protect residents from risk of injury. A notice must be displayed where all the residents can see it showing the name, address and telephone number of the manager. Landlords must ensure that main entrances shared passageways, staircases and other common areas are maintained. All services such as gas, electricity and water supplies, plus drainage facilities, must also be maintained.

The same rules apply to the internal areas of living accommodation. In addition, there is a duty to maintain adequate fire safety, as obviously, shared housing is at greater risk of fire. Self-closing fire doors, emergency escape lighting, fire alarms and detectors and fire fighting equipment will normally be required. Signs indicating fire escape routes must be displayed where they are easy to see.

There are also rules concerning overcrowding in shared housing. The local authority has powers to tackle overcrowding problems; landlords, on request, have to supply the local authority with numbers of individuals and households in a shared house. Tenants also have duties, which enable landlords to fulfil their legal responsibilities. Tenants should allow landlords access at reasonable times, give details of all who live in the accommodation, and take care to avoid damage to property.

How to register an HMO
To register an HMO, the landlord must complete a form, which can be obtained from the local authority, and also pay a fee. As stated, the license requirement will entail an extra fee.

The form requires the name and address of the landlord and the address of the property, plus:
- The name of the owner, lessee and mortgagee
- Name of the person or agent managing the property
- The number of storeys, total number of rooms in the house, number of households and number of persons occupying the house
- Details of kitchens, bathrooms, washing facilities and toilets.

Breaches of HMO regulations
If HMO regulations are breached the local authority can:

- Make landlords carry out any necessary repairs and, in extreme cases, take over the house for up to five years or make a compulsory purchase order
- Insist that the landlord provides facilities such as fire escapes and adequate amenities
- If the house is overcrowded, require the landlord to reduce the occupancy level
- Insist on access for ensuring compliance with the regulations
- Prosecute defaulting landlords
- Carry out essential work itself and recover money from the landlord.

Sanitation health and hygiene

Local authorities have a duty to serve an owner with a notice requiring the provision of WC′ when a property has insufficient sanitation, sanitation meaning toilet waste disposal.

They will also serve notice if it is thought that the existing sanitation is inadequate and is harmful to health or is a nuisance.

Local authorities have similar powers under various Public Health Acts to require owners to put right bad drains and sewers, also food storage facilities and vermin, plus the containing of disease.

The Environmental Health Department, if it considers the problem bad enough will serve a notice requiring the landlord to put the defect right. In certain cases the local authority can actually do the work and require the landlord to pay for it. This is called work *in default*.

Renovation grants

In certain cases the local authority will give assistance towards essential works on properties. Usually it is a part *grant* and is *means tested*; i.e. the amount you get depends on income.

There are different kinds of help to suit different needs, depending on the type of property involved and the scale of the work you may want to carry out.

Grants may be available towards the cost of repairs, improvements, and conversions of buildings and of providing facilities and adaptations for disabled people. In addition, minor assistance may also be available to help some tenants who want to carry out small-scale work on their homes.

There are certain circumstances where a tenant, can apply for a grant. In a lot of cases a landlord would apply because it is his/her property. The types of work which may attract grant are as follows:

Renovation grant

The main purpose for which renovation grant is intended is to bring a property up to the standard of fitness for human habitation: this includes bringing properties back up to a certain standard. Therefore typical work would be home insulation and for heating, for providing satisfactory internal arrangements and for conversions (of old houses).

The amount of grant available will be determined by the central and local government policy then in force and will almost certainly be means-tested.

Common parts grant

There is another form of grant available, the common parts grant which is applicable to blocks of flats, or houses converted into flats. Both landlord and tenant together can apply for this type of grant. Occupying tenants can apply for this grant together, without the landlord, provided that they are all liable under the terms of the tenancy agreement. Again, this grant is means-tested and is a partial grant.

There are other forms of grant available but in the main only a landlord would apply for them, such as a houses in multiple occupation grant.

In this book, there is space only or the briefest of outlines concerning the availability of grants. The first point of enquiry in relation to grants should be your local authority, which can advise you further.

Now read the Main Points from Chapter Ten

Main Points from Chapter Ten

- **Responsibility for repairs**. If a tenancy is periodic or of a fixed term for less than seven years and began after October 1961, a landlord is legally responsible for certain repairs.
- **The law**. The landlord has repairing obligations under the Landlord and Tenant Act 1985, section 11.
- **Tenants responsibility**. Normally, tenants are responsible only for minor internal repairs.
- **Landlords responsibility**. A landlord will only be responsible for a repair if it has been reported.
- **Local authority**. If a landlord does not carry out repairs then the local authority in particular the Environmental Health Department can get involved.
- **Inconvenience**. A tenant has certain rights whilst repairs are being done, particularly for inconvenience.
- **Improvements**. A tenant will not normally have the right to make improvements. However, they are entitled to certain basic amenities, such as a shower or a bath.
- **Disabled**. A disabled tenant may need certain items of equipment in their home. The local authority can advise and assist in this area, even helping with payment.
- **Shared housing**. There are special laws governing housing in multiple occupation (shared housing) particularly in relation to health and safety. The local authority can advise.

- **Local authority grants.** Private tenants may be entitled to a grant to help with work on a property. The local authority will advise on entitlement.

PART 4

RENT, SERVICE CHARGES AND INCOME TAX

11

LETTING PROPERTIES-RENT AND SERVICE CHARGES

In the following two chapters we will look at the payment of rent and the landlord and tenants obligations with regard to rent and service charges.

Depending on the type of property owned, the issue of service charges (or maintenance charges as they are sometimes misleadingly called) can be complicated, particularly for the new landlord who knows very little about the economics and legislation underpinning property management..

The payment of rent and other financial matters

If a tenancy is protected under the Rent Act 1977, as described earlier there is the right to apply to the Rent Officer for the setting of a fair rent for the property.

The assured tenant

The assured (shorthold) tenant has far fewer rights in relation to rent control than the protected tenant.

The Housing Act 1988 allows a landlord to charge whatever he likes. There is no right to a fair or reasonable rent with an assured tenancy. The rent can sometimes be negotiated at the outset of the tenancy. This rent has to be paid as long as the contractual term of the tenancy lasts. Once the contractual term has expired, the landlord is entitled to continue to charge the same rent.

On expiry of an assured shorthold the landlord is free to grant a new tenancy and set the rent to a level that is compatible with the market.

Rent control for assured shorthold tenants

We have seen that the assured shorthold tenancy is for a period of six months minimum. Like the assured tenant, the assured shorthold tenant has no right to request that a fair rent should be set. The rent is a market rent.

As with an assured tenancy, the assured shorthold tenant has the right to appeal to a Rent Assessment Committee in the case of what he/she considers an unreasonable rent. This may be done during the contractual term of the tenancy. The Committee will consider whether the rent is significantly higher than is usual for a similar property.

If the Committee assess a different rent from that set by the landlord, they may set a date when the increase will take effect. The rent cannot be backdated to before the date of the application. Once a decision has been reached by the Committee, the landlord cannot increase the rent for at least twelve months, or on termination of the tenancy.

Council tax and the tenant

From April 1993 the council tax replaced the poll tax. Unlike poll tax, the council tax is based on properties, or dwellings, and not individual people. This means that there is one bill for each individual dwelling, rather than separate bills for each person. The number and type of people who live in the dwelling may affect the size of the final bill. A discount of 25% is given for people who live alone. Each property is placed in a valuation band with different properties paying more or less depending on their individual value. Tenants who feel that their home has been placed in the wrong valuation band can appeal to their local authority council tax department.

Who has to pay the council tax?

In most cases the tenant occupying the dwelling will have to pay the council tax. However, a landlord will be responsible for paying the council tax where there are several households living in one dwelling. This will usually be hostels, bedsits and other non-self contained flats where people share things such as cooking and washing facilities. The council tax on this type of property remains the responsibility of the landlord even if all but one of the tenants move out.

Although the landlord has the responsibility for paying the council tax, he or she will normally try to pass on the increased cost through rents. However, there is a set procedure for a landlord to follow if he/she wishes to increase rent.

Dwellings, which are exempt

Certain properties will be exempt from the council tax, such as student's halls of residences and nurse's homes. Properties with all students resident will be exempt from the tax. However, if one non-student moves in then that property will no longer be exempt from tax. Uninhabitable empty properties are exempt from tax, as they are not counted as dwellings.

This is not the same as homes, which have been declared as unfit for human habitation by Environmental Health officers.

The deciding factor will be whether or not a property is capable of being lived in.

Reductions in council tax bills

Tenants in self-contained accommodation who live alone will be entitled to a discount of 25% of the total bill. Tenants may also qualify for the discount if they share their homes with people who do not count for council tax purposes. Such people are: children under eighteen; students; patients resident in hospital; people who are severely mentally impaired; low paid careworkers; eighteen or nineteen year olds still at school (or just left); people in prison (except for non-payment of fines or the council tax); and people caring for someone with a disability who is not a spouse, partner or child under eighteen.

Benefits available for those on low income

Tenants on very low income, except for students, will usually be able to claim council tax benefit. This can cover up to 100% of the council tax. Tenants with disabilities may be entitled to further discounts. Tenants who are not responsible for individual council tax, but pay it through their rent, can claim housing benefit to cover the increase. The rules covering council tax liability can be obtained from a Citizens Advice Bureau or from your local authority council tax department.

SERVICE CHARGES
What is a service charge?

A service charge covers provision of services other than those covered by the rent. A rental payment will normally cover maintenance charges, loan charges if any, and also profit.

Other services, such as cleaning and gardening, will be covered by a separate charge, known as a service charge. A *registered* rent reflects the cost of any services provided by the landlord. An assured rent set by a landlord will normally include services, which must be outlined in the agreement.

The fact that the charges are variable must be written into a tenancy agreement and the landlord has a legal duty to provide the tenant with annual budgets and accounts and has to consult when he or she wishes to spend over a certain amount of money, currently £250 per dwelling for major works such as decorating or £100 if the renewing a contract such as gardening, cleaning or lift maintenance. per scheme (estate or block of flats), whichever is the greater.

The form of consultation, which must take place, is that of writing to all those affected and informing them of:

-The landlord's intention to carry out work (30 days notice)

-Why these works are seen to be necessary;

-The estimated cost of the works (further 30 days notice)

-At least two estimates or the inviting of them to see two estimates.

The landlord can incur reasonable expense, without consultation, if the work is deemed to be necessary, i.e. emergency works.

If a service charge is variable then a landlord has certain legal obligations, which are clearly laid out in the 1985 and 1987 Landlord and Tenant Acts as amended by the 1996 Housing Act and the 2002 Commonhold and Leasehold reform Act. If you intend to let property for profit then it is of the utmost importance that you understand the law governing service charges.

Deposits

A landlord can charge a *deposit,* to set against the possibility that a tenant may damage the property or furniture. For most types of tenancy the law puts a limit on the amount that can be charged. The normal amount is 1 month's rent.

Now read the Main Points from Chapter Eleven.

Main Points from chapter Eleven

- **Fair rent**. If a tenancy is protected under the Rent Act 1977 there will be entitlement to a fair rent set by a Rent Officer.
- **Increase of fair rent**. Once the Rent Officer has set a fair rent the landlord cannot increase it unless he appeals.
- **Putting the rent up**. Even if the fair rent is higher than the existing rent, the landlord cannot charge more until the expiry of the two-year period.
- **Assured tenancies**. If a tenancy is assured there will not be the protection of the 1977 Rent Act and no entitlement to a fair rent. The rent charged would be a market rent.
- **Council tax**. If the tenant does not receive an individual bill for council tax then the landlord will be responsible for payment. This is usually the case in a multi-occupied home or block. The landlord cannot increase the rent without either notifying the Rent Officer or giving the required notice if an assured tenant.
- **Service charge**. A service charge is a charge for services such as cleaning or gardening. A landlord must show the cost of services clearly except if the total charge is less than 5% of rent. The service charge can be variable, e.g., varied once a year, or fixed, where it cannot be increased until the end of the two-year period10
- **Premiums**. It is an offence under the 1977 Rent Act to

charge a premium for granting a protected tenancy or restricted contract.

- **Deposits**. A landlord can charge a reasonable deposit for a dwelling

12

INCOME TAX

....

Rent received by a landlord is treated as income for tax purposes. The basis upon which tax is assessed is to some extent dependent on whether or not the property is furnished or unfurnished. However, these differences in taxation are unlikely to have any affect on the way that the small landlord is taxed. Agents who receive rent on a landlord's behalf can be required to pay a proportion to the Inland Revenue on account of the tax liability. This arrangement will largely depend on the landlords previous tax history. If such a direction is made then the agent must comply. If the tenant lives abroad then the tenant is under a legal obligation to deduct basic rate income tax from the rent and pay it to the Inland Revenue.

Exemptions from tax

Where the landlord lets rooms in his own home a certain amount of rent, currently £4500 per annum is exempt from tax. If there is more than one landlord, such as a couple who share the home this allowance is split between them. They cannot both claim the allowance. The amounts and details should be checked with the Inland Revenue as it is liable to either increase or decrease each year..

Deductions from tax

Expenditure from the property can be deducted from the rental income to arrive at a final figure on which tax must be paid. The following are all deductible:

- Insuring the property

- Repairs and maintenance

- Agents fees or commission

- Water rates

- Council tax

- Any rent paid to a superior landlord, such a crevice charges etc.

- Legal fees

- Interest paid on loans secured on the property, i.e., mortgages, although there are exceptions to this.

Improvements, as opposed to repairs, carried out on the property are not deductible. In practice, unless an enormous allowance is claimed, the Inland Revenue are not likely to enquire too much about this.

Payment of housing benefit directly to the landlord

Housing benefit is a payment made to the tenant rather than the landlord. The Amount of benefit that a tenant is paid will very much depend on that persons circumstances. The rules regarding payment of housing benefit have tightened considerably over the years and if you know that a tenant is going to be claiming housing benefit then you should be sure that they will be entitled. Local authorities have local rents that they will pay and they will not pay, for example, for a single person to occupy accommodation surplus to their needs or for anyone to claim what they see as excessive rent.

It is possible to arrange for the local authority to pay housing benefit direct to the landlord, especially where there are more than eight weeks in arrears. If there is an arrears problem and the landlord believes that the tenant is entitled to, or may be receiving housing benefit then the local authority should be contacted.

Housing benefit and possession for arrears of rent

Very often, problems in obtaining benefit will cause tenants to accrue rent arrears. If a landlord has let a property knowing that the tenant is claiming housing benefit it is better to wait for the tenant to sort it out. The court is unlikely to give possession if arrears are accruing because of benefit. Once there are eight weeks of arrears (see grounds for possession) then the court has no choice but to give possession anyway and quite often it is better to wait rather than jumping the gun and losing rental income altogether.

If on the other hand the tenant has stated that they are going to pay rent personally rather than benefit then the court will look more favorably on- giving possession to the landlord if arrears have arisen as a result of an immediate claim for benefit.

Now read the Main points from Chapter Twelve

Main points from Chapter Twelve

- Rent received by a landlord is treated as income for tax purposes. The basis on which tax is assessed is dependant on whether or not the property is furnished or unfurnished.

- Agents who receive income on a landlord's behalf can be required to pay a proportion to the Inland Revenue depending on that persons tax history.

- Where the landlord lets rooms in his own home, a certain amount of rent, currently approximately £4500 per annum is exempt from tax. This should be checked with the Inland Revenue.

- There are a number of items that are tax deductible, such as repairs and insurance, agents fees ad commissions, water rates and so on.

- Housing benefit is a payment made to a tenant rather than the landlord. However, it is essential that you sign a form to say that the actual payment should come direct to the landlord.

13

PRIVATE TENANCIES IN SCOTLAND

....

The law governing the relationship between private landlords and tenants in Scotland is different to that in England. Since the beginning of 1989, new private sector tenancies in Scotland have been covered by the Housing (Scotland) Act 1988. Following the passage of this Act, private sector tenants no longer have any protection as far as rent levels are concerned and tenants enjoy less security of tenure.

There are four essential elements in the creation of a tenancy under Scottish law:

- An agreement between landlord and tenant
- The payment of rent. If someone is allowed to occupy a property without an agreement then this will not amount to a tenancy
- A fixed permission date (called an 'ish')
- Possession

The agreement must be in writing if the tenancy is for a period of 1 year or more. Agreements of less than a year can be oral.

Different types of tenancy
There are different tenancy types in the private sector,

differing according to when they were entered into. In the case of assured tenancies they will differ depending on what landlord and tenant agreed between themselves. The different types of tenancy are:

- Protected tenancy
- Statutory tenancy
- Assured tenancy
- Short assured tenancy.

Protected tenancies

Before 1989, most private sector tenancies were likely to be protected tenancies. A protected tenancy is a contractual tenancy covered by the Rent Act (Scotland) 1984 and must satisfy the following requirements:

- The house must be let as a dwelling house (this can apply to a house or part of a house)
- The house must be a separate dwelling
- The ratable value must be less than a specified sum

Various categories of dwellings did not qualify as protected tenancies. A protected tenancy retains its status until the death of a tenant or his spouse, or any eligible successor, and therefore some protected tenancies are still in existence today.

Grounds for possession

As is the case in England and Wales, where there is no protected tenancy, the landlord may possess a property only by obtaining a court order. The landlord must serve a notice to quit, giving 28 days notice. A ground for possession must be shown, either discretionary or mandatory before possession can be given.

The grounds for possession are similar to those in England and Wales, with ten mandatory and ten discretionary grounds applying.

Fair rent system

A fair rent system, similar to England and Wales, exists in Scotland for protected tenants. There is a set procedure to be followed, with either the landlord or tenant, or jointly, making an application to the rent officer. Once fixed, the rent is valid for three years. A fresh application can be made within three years if circumstances relating to the tenancy radically alter, such as a substantial refurbishment.

Statutory tenancies

A statutory tenancy is one which arises when a tenant remains in possession of a house after the contractual tenancy has been terminated (e.g. by a notice to quit) or a tenant has previously succeeded to the tenancy before 1990. A statutory tenant has similar rights to a protected tenant.

Assured tenants

Under the Housing (Scotland) Act 1988, the assured tenancy was introduced into Scotland coming into force after 2nd January 1989. This is very similar indeed to the assured tenancy introduced into England and Wales in 1989.

A Scottish assured tenancy has three elements:
- the tenancy must be of a house or flat or self contained

dwelling. For an agreement to exist, there must be an agreement, rent payable a termination date and possession, as there is in all leases in Scotland

- The house must be let as a separate dwelling. A tenancy may be of a flat, part of a house, or even a single room, provided it is possible for the tenant to carry on all 'the major activities of residential life there, i.e. sleeping, cooking and feeding.
- The tenant must be an individual. A company cannot be given an assured tenancy

The list of exclusions from assured tenancy status are the same as those in England and all the other provisions concerning rent, sub-letting succession, security of tenure and so on, apply.

The grounds for possession and the law governing termination of tenancies is a reflection of English Law.

Short assured tenancies

The Housing Act (Scotland) also introduced 'short assured tenancies', a distinct form of assured tenancy for a fixed term of six months. Again, this is a reflection of the assured shorthold with the same provisions applying. The short assured tenant has little security of tenure. See appendix for example tenancy and notice (AT5) which must be served on the tenant prior to entering into the agreement stating that the agreement is a short assured tenancy.

The following are the conditions for the creation of a short assured tenancy:

1) The tenancy fulfills the requirements of a valid assured tenancy
2) The landlord, before the creation of the tenancy, has served on the tenant a formal notice (AT5) stating that the proposed tenancy is to be a short assured tenancy and giving various information set out in regulations
3) The tenancy is for a fixed period of not less than six-months (there is no maximum period)

One main difference between assured shorthold tenancies and short assured is that, if neither landlord nor tenant take any action to renew the tenancy at the end of the fixed period (6 months) then the tenancy will automatically renew for the same minimum fixed period (or one year if the fixed period was more than one year). This is known as 'tacit relocation'.

Recovery of possession

A short assured tenant has no defence to a properly based possession action. The sheriff must grant an order for possession if he is satisfied that all of the following apply:
1) The tenancy has reached its termination date
2) No tacit relocation is in action (i.e. a valid notice to quit of at least 40 days has been served by the landlord
3) No further contractual tenancy is in existence
4) The landlord has given at least two months notice to the tenant that he requires possession of the house. The notice can be served during the tenancy or after the termination date.

As with the English Assured shorthold, the landlord does not need to give any reason why he needs possession. In addition, because the short assured tenancy is a type of assured tenancy then recovery using the grounds for possession is the same as the assured tenancy.

It can be seen that, apart from a number of minor differences, there are many similarities between the assured shorthold and the short assured tenancy.

Now read the main points from Chapter 13

Main points from Chapter 13

- Private sector tenancies in Scotland are regulated by the Housing (Scotland act 1998)

- Agreements of 1 year or more must be in writing. Agreements for less than 1 year can be verbal.

- The most common form of private sector tenancy is the short assured tenancy

- There are many similarities between the short assured tenancy and the assured shorthold tenancy

14

ADVICE FOR TENANTS

....

Although this guide is aimed at landlords, or prospective landlords, it is important not to forget the tenant, the person who makes rental investments possible. The relationship between landlord and tenant is not based solely on the law but is also based on common decency and understanding. Landlords will also find the following advice useful when contemplating letting out properties.

If you are a tenant viewing prospective apartments it is important to understand that the property, unless otherwise stated, is 'as seen'. Generally speaking, items that are not included in an inventory are not available to the tenant.

Once you have chosen the property that you want to make your home, the next step is to provide the landlord or agent with satisfactory references. Most agencies will require references from your bank, a previous landlord or agent and a personal reference usually from an employer. These will be applied for directly so they cannot be faked.

Some agencies use a credit reference agency for this purpose and there may be a charge for this.

Guarantees

In some cases, particularly if the tenant is on benefits, the landlord will require rental payment guarantees, and this involves getting someone to act as a guarantor. This will be someone who is prepared to stand as guarantor for the rent for the entire duration of the tenancy, including any renewals and extensions. For many tenants this has proved a sticking point as it is quite a lot to ask anyone.

However, provided that both you and the references are suitable, and any guarantees are in place, the next step will be to draw up a tenancy agreement. This should be read very thoroughly including the small print. Do not sign anything that you are not happy with.

Once the agreement has been entered into it is returned to the landlord or agent with a holding deposit of (usually) £200 to secure the tenancy which is deducted from the final amount handed over.

Before the tenancy commences. You will receive an invoice detailing all monies to be paid over before you take possession. These include:

- The initial rent, usually one month, depending on the terms of the agreement
- The deposit, which will usually be one months rent. The deposit covers dilapidations and damage
- The inventory contribution fee. Usually, unless the tenant is a company, the landlord will pay for the inventory
- The credit reference fee if applicable

- The tenancy agreement fee. This is non-refundable should you, for any reason, decide not to proceed with the tenancy. Most agencies will only charge the tenant for the agreement if it deviates in important ways from the assured shorthold agreement, i.e. if the tenancy is for a short let, if it is for a company let, or if the rent exceeds a certain figure per annum which puts it outside an assured shorthold.

On the day the tenancy commences the landlord or agent will check you into the property, You will need to sign a form as to the condition of the property. Meter readings should be taken at the check in and the landlord or agent concerned will notify the various utilities companies of the change. Sometimes this does not happen and it is important that the tenant does this.

Remember, your landlord is responsible for most repairs and it is important that you notify him or the agent immediately when there is a problem. The landlord is only responsible once notified of a problem.

Useful addresses and websites

Association of Residential Letting agencies (ARLA)
ARLA Administration
Maple House
53-55 Woodside Road
Amersham
Bucks HP6 6AA
Hotline 01923 896555

Tel: 01923 896555
Website: www.arla.co.uk
Email: info@arla.co.uk

Court Service
Southside
105 Victoria Street
London SW1E 6QF
0207 210 2266
www.courtservice.gov.uk
Email customerservice@courtservice.gsi.gov.uk

Leasehold Advisory Service
70-74 City Road
London EC1Y 2BJ
0207490 9580
Fax: 0207 253 2043
www.lease-advice.org
Email info@lease-advice.org

GLOSSARY OF TERMS

A SUMMARY OF IMPORTANT TERMS

FREEHOLDER: Someone who owns their property outright.

LEASEHOLDER: Someone who has been granted permission to live on someone else's land for a fixed term.

TENANCY: One form of lease, the most common types of which are fixed-term or periodic.

LANDLORD: A person who owns the property in which the tenant lives.

LICENCE: A license is an agreement entered into whereby the landlord is merely giving you permission to occupy his/her property for a limited period of time.

TRESPASSER: Someone who has no right through an agreement to live in a property.

PROTECTED TENANT: In the main, subject to certain exclusions, someone whose tenancy began before 15th January 1989.

ASSURED TENANT: In the main, subject to certain exclusions, someone whose tenancy began after 15th January 1989.

NOTICE TO QUIT: A legal document giving the protected

tenant twenty eight days notice that the landlord intends to apply for possession of the property to the County Court.

GROUND FOR POSSESSION: One of the stated reasons for which the landlord can apply for possession of the property.

MANDATORY GROUND: Where the judge must give possession of the property.

DISCRETIONARY GROUND: Where the judge may or may not give possession, depending on his own opinion.

STUDENT LETTING: A tenancy granted by a specified educational institution.

HOLIDAY LETTING: A dwelling used for holiday purposes only.

ASSURED SHORTHOLD TENANCY: A fixed-term post-1989 tenancy.

PAYMENT OF RENT: Where you pay a regular sum of money in return for permission to occupy a property or land for a specified period of time.

FAIR RENT: A rent set by the Rent Officer every two years for most pre-1989 tenancies and which is lower than a market rent.

MARKET RENT: A rent deemed to be comparable with other non-fair rents in the area.

RENT ASSESSMENT COMMITTEE: A committee set up to review rents set by either the Rent Officer or the landlord.

PREMIUM: A sum of money charged for permission to live in a property.

DEPOSIT: A sum of money held against the possibility of damage to property.

QUIET ENJOYMENT: The right to live peacefully in own home.
REPAIRS: Work required to keep a property in good order.

IMPROVEMENTS: Alterations to a property.

LEGAL AID: Help with your legal costs, which is dependent on income.

HOUSING BENEFIT: Financial help with rent, which is dependent on income.

HOUSING ADVICE CENTRE: A center which exists to give advice on housing-related matters and which is usually local authority-funded.

LAW CENTRE: A center, which exists for the purpose of assisting the public with legal advice.

INDEX

Advice for tenants 125
Advertisement   44
Appeal 74
(Rent Officer decision)   74
Assured
(Tenancy)   71 105
(Shorthold)   16 65 70

Bedsits 49
Benefit
(Housing)   48
Budget   11
Business
(Plan) 11 15 18
(Tenancy) 34
Buying a listed building 27
Buying a property   33
Buying a new home 28
Buying property at auction 35

Choosing your property 24
Conservation areas 29
Considerations when buying a property 19
Conveyancing costs   12
Committee
(Rent Assessment)   80
Company
(Lets)   45
Compensation
    (Quiet enjoyment)   83

Contract
(Tenancy)   53
Court 99
Council Tax 106

Damages 85
Deposit 11 110
Deterioration
(Of premises)   93
Disrepair 93
Disabled
(Tenant) 96

Emergency works 94
End of tenancy 55
Environmental Health
(Department) 87
Eviction 75
Exchange of contracts 34
Explaining the law 59
Exemptions from tax 113
Extending a lease 26

Fair rent 80
Fast track possession 80
Finding a tenant 41
Freehold 60
Furniture 53

Grant
(Renovation) 96

Grounds
(For possession) 76

Housing Benefit   48 115
Holiday lets   48
Houses in multi-occupation 98
Housing law 53

Injunctions   85
Income tax   113
Improvements   96
Insurance   55

Joint Tenancies   80

Land Registry   13
Lease 61
Leasehold 61
Letting agents   42
Leasehold Reform Act 1993   26
Looking for a property 23

Making an offer   33
Market Rent 73
Mortgage fees   15
Mortgage indemnity insurance 15

Notice
(To quit/seeking possession)   62
Negative equity 13

Overcrowding 65

Protected Tenant
(Rent Act)   47
Possession of property 74 89
Preparing for auction 35
Preparing to purchase a flat 25
Provisions under a tenancy 53
Public sector   44
Purchasing property for investment 11

Quiet
(Enjoyment) 83

Renovation grant   100
Rent   80 105
Rental guarantees 50
Repairs   93

Sale by tender 37
Sanitation 99
Scotland 117
Searches   13
Security of tenure   76
Seller's pack 33
Services   54
Service charges   105 108
Shared housing   97
Short lets   46
Squatter   66
Stamp duty   12

Structural surveys   13
Students   47

Tenancy running on 75
The tenancy agreement   62
The tenant   61
The 1988 Housing Act 15
The 1996 Housing Act 25
Trespasser   59

Viewing a property 26

APPENDIX

1.Typical residential tenancy agreement (England)

2.Notice requiring possession of an assured shorthold tenancy.

3. Tenancy agreement (Scotland)

4. Landlords notice to terminate (Scotland)

5. Example Inventory

ENGLAND & WALES

ASSURED SHORTHOLD TENANCY AGREEMENT

Notes for Guidance		
Insert date of agreement.	Dated	_____
The address of the property to be let. For shared properties, be sure to identify clearly the tenant's room or part of the property, e.g. by giving it a number.	The Property (hereinafter called 'the Property')	_____ _____ ~ _____ _____ _____
The landlord should give here an address in England and Wales.	The Landlord (hereinafter called 'the Landlord')	_____ of _____ _____
		This is the Landlord's address for service of notices until the Tenant is notified of a different address in England and Wales.
Insert full name(s), and address(es) (if relevant) of every tenant.	The Tenant (hereinafter called 'the Tenant')	_____ of _____ _____
		Where the Tenant consists of more than one person, they will all have joint and several liability under this agreement (this means that they will each be liable for **all** sums due under this Agreement, not just liable for a proportionate part).
Insert name and address of guarantor. Delete if none.	The Guarantor (hereinafter called 'the Guarantor')	_____ of _____ _____
Insert period of term in weeks/months and date tenancy begins. * *Delete as applicable depending on whether rent is to be paid monthly or weekly.*	The Term	_____ beginning on _____ ('the fixed period') The tenancy will then continue, still subject to the terms and conditions set out in this Agreement, from month to month/week to week * from the end of this fixed period unless or until the Tenant gives notice that he wishes to end the Agreement as set out in clause 4 overleaf, or the Landlord serves on the Tenant a notice under Section 21 of the Housing Act 1988, or a new form of Agreement is entered into, or this Agreement is ended by consent or a court order.
* *Delete as applicable. NB If rent is paid weekly, a rent book must be provided to the tenant.*	The Rent	£_____ per calendar month/week * by way of standing order into the Landlord's bank, details of which have been provided to the Tenant*.
† *If paid weekly, give the day in the week, e.g. Monday.*	The Payment Date	The first payment to be made on the signing of this Agreement. All subsequent payments to be made monthly/weekly * in advance on the _____ day of the month/ _____ of each week *†.
NB The deposit should not exceed two months' rent.	The Deposit	£ _____ The deposit to be held as security by the Landlord for any loss or damage caused by the breach of any of the Tenant's obligations under this Agreement, or any sum repayable by the Landlord to the Local Authority in respect of Housing Benefit paid direct to the Landlord. See also clause 5 overleaf.
Delete this section if there is no inventory.	The Inventory	Being the list of the Landlord's possessions at the Property and details of condition which has been signed by the Landlord and the Tenant, a copy of which is annexed hereto.

This Agreement is intended to create an assured shorthold tenancy as defined in the Housing Act 1988, as amended by the Housing Act 1996, and the provisions for the recovery of possession by the Landlord in that Act apply accordingly. The Tenant understands that the Landlord will be entitled to recover possession of the Property at the end of the Term.

[Under this Agreement, the Tenant will have exclusive occupation of his designated room and will share with other occupiers of the Property the use and facilities of the Property (including such bathroom, toilet, kitchen and sitting room facilities as may be at the Property).]

1. The Tenant's obligations:

1.1 To pay the Rent at the times and in the manner aforesaid.

1.2 [To pay all charges in respect of any electric, gas, water, telephonic and televisual services used at or supplied to the Property and Council Tax or any similar property tax that might be charged in addition to or replacement of it during the Term.] [To make a proportionate contribution to the costs of all charges in respect of any electric, gas, water and telephone or televisual services used at or supplied to the Property and Council Tax or any similar property tax that might be charged in addition to or replacement of it during the Term.]

1.3 To keep the items on the Inventory and the interior of the Property in a good and clean state and condition and not damage or injure the Property or the items on the Inventory (fair wear and tear excepted).

1.4 To yield up the Property and the items on the Inventory (if any) at the end of the Term in the same clean state and condition it/they was/were in at the beginning of the Term (but the Tenant will not be responsible for fair wear and tear caused during normal use of the Property, and the items on the Inventory or for any damage covered by and recoverable under the insurance policy effected by the Landlord under clause 2.2).

1.5 Not make any alteration or addition to the Property nor without the Landlord's prior written consent (consent not to be withheld unreasonably) do any redecoration or painting of the Property.

1.6 Not do anything on or at the Property which:

1.6.1 may be or become a nuisance or annoyance to any other occupiers of the Property or owners or occupiers of adjoining or nearby premises

1.6.2 is illegal or immoral

1.6.3 may in any way affect the validity of the insurance of the Property and the items listed on the Inventory or cause an increase in the premium payable by the Landlord.

1.7 Not without the Landlord's prior consent (consent not to be withheld unreasonably) allow or keep any pet or any kind of animal at the Property.

1.8 Not use or occupy the Property in any way whatsoever other than as a private residence.

1.9 Not to assign, sublet, charge or part with or share possession or occupation of the Property (but see clause 4.1 below).

1.10 To allow the Landlord or anyone with the Landlord's written permission to enter the Property at reasonable times of the day to inspect its condition and state of repair, carry out any necessary repairs and gas inspections, or during the last month of the Term, show the Property to prospective new tenants, provided the Landlord has given 24 hours' prior written notice (except in emergency).

1.11 To pay the Landlord's reasonable costs reasonably incurred as a result of any breaches by the Tenant of his obligations under this Agreement.

1.12 To pay interest at the rate of 4% above the Bank of England base rate from time to time prevailing on any rent or other money due from the Tenant which remains unpaid for more that 14 days, interest to be paid from the date the payment fell due until payment.

1.13 To provide the Landlord with a forwarding address when the tenancy comes to an end and to remove all rubbish and all personal items (including the Tenant's own furniture and equipment) from the Property before leaving.

2. The Landlord's obligations:

2.1 The Landlord agrees that the Tenant may live in the Property without unreasonable interruption from the Landlord or any person rightfully claiming under or in trust for the Landlord.

2.2 To insure the Property and the items listed on the Inventory and use all reasonable efforts to arrange for any damage caused by an insured risk to be remedied as soon as possible and to provide a copy of the insurance policy to the Tenant.

2.3 To keep in repair

2.3.1 the structure and exterior of the Property (including drains, gutters and external pipes)

2.3.2 the installations at the Property for the supply of water, gas and electricity and for sanitation (including basins, sinks, baths and sanitary conveniences), and

2.3.3 the installations at the Property for space heating and heating water.

2.4 But the Landlord will not be required to:

2.4.1 carry out works for which the Tenant is responsible by virtue of his duty to use the Property in a tenant-like manner

2.4.2 reinstate the Property in the case of damage or destruction if the insurers refuse to pay out the insurance money due to anything the Tenant has done or failed to do

2.4.3 rebuild or reinstate the Property in the case of destruction or damage of the Property by a risk not covered by the policy of insurance effected by the Landlord.

3. Guarantor

If there is a Guarantor, he guarantees that the Tenant will keep to his obligations in this agreement. The Guarantor agrees to pay on demand to the Landlord any money lawfully due to the Landlord by the Tenant.

4. Ending this Agreement

4.1 The Tenant cannot normally end this Agreement before the end of the Term. However, after the first three months of the Term, if the Tenant can find a suitable alternative tenant, and provided this alternative tenant is acceptable to the Landlord (the Landlord's approval not to be unreasonably withheld) the Tenant may give notice to end the tenancy on a date at least one month from the date that such approval is given by the Landlord. On the expiry of such notice, provided that the Tenant pays to the Landlord the reasonable expenses reasonably incurred by the Landlord in granting the necessary approval and in granting any new tenancy to the alternative tenant, the tenancy shall end.

4.2 If the Tenant stays on after the end of the fixed Term, his tenancy will continue but will run from [month to month]|[week to week] (a 'periodic tenancy'). This periodic tenancy can be ended by the Tenant giving at least one month's written notice to the Landlord, the notice to expire at the end of a rental period.

4.3 If at any time

4.3.1 any part of the Rent is outstanding for 21 days after becoming due (whether formally demanded or not) and/or

4.3.2 there is any breach, non-observance or non-performance by the Tenant of any covenant or other term of this Agreement which has been notified in writing to the Tenant and the Tenant has failed within a reasonable period of time to remedy the breach and/or pay reasonable compensation to the Landlord for the breach and/or

4.3.3 any of the grounds set out as Grounds 2, 8 or Grounds 10-15 (inclusive) (which relate to breach of any obligation by a Tenant) contained in the Housing Act 1988 Schedule 2 apply

the Landlord may recover possession of the Property and this Agreement shall come to an end. The Landlord retains all his other rights in respect of the Tenant's obligations under this Agreement. Note that if anyone is living at the Property or if the tenancy is an assured or assured shorthold tenancy then the Landlord must obtain a court order for possession before re-entering the Property. This clause does not affect the Tenant's rights under the Protection from Eviction Act 1977.

5. **The Deposit**

5.1 The Deposit will be held by the Landlord and will be refunded to the Tenant at the end of the Term (however it ends) at the forwarding address provided to the Landlord but less any reasonable deductions properly made by the Landlord to cover any reasonable costs incurred or losses caused to him by any breaches of the obligations in this Agreement by the Tenant. No interest will be payable to the Tenant in respect of the deposit money.

5.2 The Deposit shall be repayable to the Tenant as soon as reasonably practicable, however the Landlord shall not be bound to return the deposit until he is satisfied that no money is repayable to the Local Authority if the Tenant has been in receipt of Housing Benefit, and until after he has had a reasonable opportunity to assess the reasonable cost of any repairs required as a result of any breaches of his obligations by the Tenant or other sums properly due to the Landlord under clause 5.1. However, the Landlord shall not, save in exceptional circumstances, retain the Deposit for more than one month after the end of the tenancy.

5.3 If at any time during the Term the Landlord is obliged to deduct from the Deposit to satisfy the reasonable costs occasioned by any breaches of the obligations of the Tenant, the Tenant shall make such additional payments as are necessary to restore the full amount of the Deposit.

6. **Other provisions**

6.1 The Landlord hereby notifies the Tenant under Section 48 of the Landlord & Tenant Act 1987 that any notices (including notices in proceedings) should be served upon the Landlord at the address stated with the name of the Landlord overleaf.

6.2 For stamp duty purposes, the Landlord and the Tenant confirm that there is no previous agreement to which this Agreement gives effect.

6.3 The Landlord shall be entitled to have and retain keys for all the doors to the Property but shall not be entitled to use these to enter the Property without the consent of the Tenant (save in an emergency).

6.4 Any notices or other documents shall be deemed served on the Tenant during the tenancy by either being left at the Property or by being sent to the Tenant at the Property by first-class post. If notices or other documents are served on the Tenant by post they shall be deemed served on the day after posting.

6.5 Any person other than the Tenant who pays all or part of the rent due under this Agreement to the Landlord shall be deemed to have made such payment as agent for and on behalf of the Tenant which the Landlord shall be entitled to assume without enquiry.

6.6 Any personal items left behind at the end of the tenancy after the Tenant has vacated (which the Tenant has not removed in accordance with clause 1.13 of this Agreement) shall be considered abandoned if they have not been removed within 14 days of written notice to the Tenant from the Landlord or if the Landlord has been unable to trace the Tenant by taking reasonable steps to do so. After this period the Landlord may remove or dispose of the items as he thinks fit. The Tenant shall be liable for the reasonable disposal costs which may be deducted from the proceeds of sale (if any), and the Tenant shall remain liable for any balance. Any net proceeds of sale will be dealt with in the same way as the Deposit as set out in clause 5.2 above.

6.7 In the event of damage to or destruction of the Property by any of the risks insured against by the Landlord the Tenant shall be relieved from payment of the Rent to the extent that the Tenant's use and enjoyment of the Property is thereby prevented and from performance of its obligations as to the state and condition of the Property to the extent of and so long as there prevails such damage or destruction (except to the extent that the insurance is prejudiced by any act or default of the Tenant).

6.8 Where the context so admits:

6.8.1 The 'Landlord' includes the persons from time to time entitled to receive the Rent.

6.8.2 The 'Tenant' includes any persons deriving title under the Tenant.

6.8.3 The 'Property' includes any part or parts of the Property and all of the Landlord's fixtures and fittings at or upon the Property.

6.8.4 All references to the singular shall include the plural and vice versa and any obligations or liabilities of more than one person shall be joint and several (this means that they will each be liable for *all* sums due under this Agreement, not just liable for a proportionate part) and an obligation on the part of a party shall include an obligation not to allow or permit the breach of that obligation.

6.8.5 All references to 'he', 'him' and 'his' shall be taken to include 'she', 'her' and 'hers'.

Insert here any additional terms you would like incorporated into the Agreement.

Additional provisions (if any)

_____

_____

_____

_____

_____

_____

_____

_____

_____

_____

_____

_____

_____

_____

_____

_____

_____

_____

_____

_____

Landlord signs here **Landlord's signature** _____

Witness (if any) signs here **Witness's signature** _____

All tenants sign here **Tenant's signature(s)** _____

_____

_____

_____

Witness (if any) signs here **Witness's signature** _____

Guarantor signs here (if any) **Guarantor's signature** _____

Witness signs here **Witness's signature** _____

ENGLAND & WALES
HOUSING ACT 1988
Section 21

Assured Shorthold Tenancy : Notice Requiring Possession

Notes for Guidance

Name & address of Tenant

To _____

of _____

_____

Name & address of Landlord

From _____

of _____

_____

Address of dwelling

I/We* give you notice that I/we* require possession of the dwelling house known as

_____

Expiry date

after _____

or (if this notice would otherwise be invalid) I/we* require possession on the first date after:

- at least two months after service upon you of this notice, and

- (if your tenancy is for a fixed period) a date not earlier than the end of the fixed period, or

- (if your tenancy is a periodic tenancy) the last date of a period of your tenancy but no earlier than the date on which your tenancy could lawfully be ended by a notice to quit

Dated _____

Delete as applicable

Signed _____ Landlord/Landlord's agent*

Name address & telephone number of agent if the form is signed by the Landlord's agent

_____

_____

_____

PRESCRIBED INFORMATION

As set out in the Notices to Quit (Prescribed Information) Regulations 1988

1. If the tenant or licensee does not leave the dwelling the landlord or licensor must get an order for possession from the court before the tenant or licensee can be lawfully evicted. The landlord or licensor cannot apply for such an order before the notice to quit or notice to determine has run out (i.e. before the expiry date).

2. A tenant or licensee who does not know if he has any right to remain in possession after a notice to quit or a notice to determine runs out can obtain advice from a solicitor. Help with all or part of the cost of legal advice may be available under the Legal Aid Scheme. He should also be able to obtain information from a Citizens Advice Bureau, a Housing Aid centre or a Rent Officer.

128

SCOTLAND
SHORT ASSURED TENANCY AGREEMENT

Notes for Guidance

Insert date of agreement.	Dated	_____
The address of the property to be let. For shared properties, be sure to identify clearly the tenant's room or part of the property, e.g. by giving it a number.	The Property (hereinafter called 'the Property')	_____
The landlord should give here an address in Scotland.	The Landlord (hereinafter called 'the Landlord')	of _____

This is the Landlord's address for service of notices until the Tenant is notified of a different address in Scotland.

Insert full name(s), and address(es) (if relevant) of every tenant.	The Tenant (hereinafter called 'the Tenant')	of _____

Where the Tenant consists of more than one person, they will all have joint and several liability under this agreement(this means that they will each be liable for all sums due under this Agreement, not just liable for a proportionate part).

Insert name and address of guarantor. Delete if none.	The Guarantor (hereinafter called 'the Guarantor')	of _____

Insert period of term in weeks/months and date tenancy begins. Initial term must be for at least 6 months.	The Term

_____ beginning on _____ ('the fixed period')

The tenancy will then continue, still subject to the terms and conditions set out in this Agreement, from the end of this fixed period unless or until the Tenant gives notice that he wishes to end the Agreement, as set out in clause 8 overleaf, or the Landlord serves on the Tenant the required notices in terms of the Housing Act (Scotland) Act 1988, or a new form of Agreement is entered into, or this Agreement is ended by consent or a Court order.

* Delete as applicable. NB If rent is paid weekly, a rent book must be provided to the tenant.	The Rent

£_____ per calendar month/week *

by way of standing order into the Landlord's bank, details of which have been provided to the Tenant*.

† If paid weekly, give the day in the week, e.g. Monday.	The Payment Date

The first payment to be made on the signing of this Agreement. All subsequent payments to be made monthly/weekly * in advance on the _____ day of the month/ _____ of each week *†.

NB The deposit should not exceed two months' rent.	The Deposit

£ _____ *

The deposit to be held as security by the Landlord for any loss or damage caused by the breach of any of the Tenant's obligations under this Agreement, or any sum repayable by the Landlord to the Local Authority in respect of Housing Benefit paid direct to the Landlord. See also clause 5 overleaf.

Delete this section if there is no inventory.	The Inventory

Being the list of the Landlord's possessions at the Property and details of condition which has been signed by the Landlord and the Tenant, a copy of which is annexed hereto.

129

Terms and Conditions

delete
paragraph if
hole property
being let.

[Under this Agreement, the Tenant will have exclusive occupation of his designated room and will share with other occupiers of the Property the use and facilities of the Property (including such bathroom, toilet, kitchen and sitting room facilities as may be at the Property).]

1. This Agreement is intended to create a short assured tenancy as defined in Section 32 of the Housing (Scotland) Act 1988 and the Tenant acknowledges that he has received prior to the creation of the Tenancy notice to that effect in Form AT5 that the tenancy may be brought to an end by an order for possession granted by the Sheriff on the application of the Landlord or of the heritable creditor of the Landlord in any of the circumstances set out in Grounds 2, 8 or 9 to 17 inclusive in Schedule 5 to the Housing (Scotland) Act 1988 provided always that the Landlord has complied with Section 19 of that Act.

2. The Tenant will:

   2.1 pay the Rent at the times and in the manner aforesaid without any deduction abatement or set-off whatsoever;

   2.2 [immediately upon occupation of the Property to arrange for the Tenant to be registered as the consumer of gas, electricity and telephone services and to pay all charges in respect of any electric, gas, water and telephonic or televisual services used at or supplied to the Property and Council Tax or any similar tax that might be charged in addition to or replacement of it during the Term;] [make a proportionate contribution to the costs of all charges in respect of any electric, gas, water and telephone or televisual services used at or supplied to the Property and Council Tax or any similar property tax that might be charged in addition to or replacement of it during the Term;]

delete sentence
which does not
apply.

   2.3 keep the interior of the Property in a good, clean and tenantable state and condition and not damage or injure the Property and take all necessary precautions against damage by frost or flooding the Tenant accepting the Property and contents (so far as belonging to the Landlord) and (save as specified in the Inventory) as being in good tenantable order and condition at the commencement of the Tenancy, the Tenant by acceptance hereof renouncing any claims against the Landlord in respect thereof;

   2.4 yield up the Property and all and any items listed on the Inventory belonging to the Landlord at the end of the Term in the same clean state and condition they were in at the beginning of the Term (reasonable wear and tear and damage by insured risks excepted);

   2.5 not install or erect fixed TV aerial or satellite dish or make any alteration or addition to the Property nor without the Landlord's prior written consent do any redecoration or painting of the Property;

   2.6 not do or omit to do anything on or at the Property which may be or become a nuisance or annoyance to the Landlord or owners or occupiers of adjoining or nearby premises or

which may in any way prejudice the insurance of the Property or cause an increase in the premium payable therefore;

   2.7 not without the Landlord's prior consent allow or keep any pet or any kind of animal at the Property;

   2.8 not leave the Property unoccupied for any period exceeding 3 weeks and not use or occupy the Property in any way whatsoever other than as a private residence;

   2.9 not assign, sublet, charge or part with or share possession or occupation of the Property;

   2.10 permit the Landlord or anyone authorised by the Landlord at reasonable hours and upon reasonable prior notice (except in emergency) to enter and view the Property for any proper purpose (including the checking of compliance with the Tenant's obligations under this Agreement and during the last month of the Term the showing of the Property to prospective new tenants);

   2.11 pay interest at the rate of 4% above the Base Lending Rate for the time being of the Landlord's bankers upon any rent or other money due from the Tenant under this Agreement which is more than 3 days in arrears in respect of the period from when it became due to the date of payment.

3. If there is a Guarantor, he guarantees that the Tenant will keep to his obligations in this Agreement. The Guarantor agrees to pay on demand to the Landlord any amount that the Tenant owes.

4. The Landlord will:

   4.1 subject to the Tenant paying the Rent and performing his obligations under this Agreement allow the Tenant peaceably to hold and enjoy the Property during the Term without lawful interruption from the Landlord or any person rightfully claiming under or in trust for the Landlord;

   4.2 insure the Property and the contents of the Property which belong to the Landlord and provide a copy of the insurance policy to the Tenant;

   4.3 keep in repair the structure and exterior of the Property (including drains, gutters and external pipes);

   4.4 keep in repair and proper working order the installations at the Property for the supply of water, gas and electricity and for sanitation (including basins, sinks, baths and sanitary conveniences);

   4.5 keep in repair and proper working order the installations at the Property for space heating and heating water.

4.6 But the Landlord will not be required to:

4.6.1 carry out works for which the Tenant is responsible by virtue of his duty to use the Property in a tenantlike manner;

4.6.2 rebuild or reinstate the Property in the case of destruction or damage by fire or by tempest flood or other accident.

5. The Deposit has been paid by the Tenant and is held by the Landlord to secure compliance with the Tenant's obligations under this Agreement (without prejudice to the Landlord's other rights and remedies) and if, at any time during the Term, the Landlord is obliged to draw upon it to satisfy any outstanding breaches of such obligations then the Tenant shall forthwith make such additional payment as is necessary to restore the full amount of the Deposit held by the Landlord. As soon as reasonably practicable following termination of this Agreement the Landlord shall return to the Tenant the Deposit or the balance thereof after any deductions properly made without interest.

6. The Landlord hereby notifies the Tenant that any notices (including notices in proceedings) should be served upon the Landlord at the address stated with the name of the Landlord overleaf.

7. In the event of damage to or destruction of the Property by any of the risks insured by the Landlord the Tenant shall be relieved from payment of the Rent to the extent that the Tenant's use and enjoyment of the Property is thereby prevented and from performance of his obligations as to the state and condition of the Property to the extent of and so long as there prevails such damage or destruction (except to the extent that the insurance is prejudiced by any act or default of the Tenant) the amount in case of dispute to be settled by arbitration.

8. This Agreement and the tenancy hereby constituted may be terminated:

8.1 by the parties at any time by mutual agreement in writing; or

8.2 by either party on or after the end of the Term by giving to the other party not less than 2 months' notice in writing of termination or such shorter period of notice as the parties may mutually agree in writing.

8.3 It is expressly agreed that if:

8.3.1 the rent or any part thereof shall be unpaid for 14 days after any of the Rent Payment Dates whether demanded or not; or

8.3.2 any other sum due and payable by the Tenant to the Landlord under this Agreement shall be unpaid for 14 days after the date on which it falls due and payable in terms of the relevant provision hereof; or

8.3.3 there shall be any other breach, non-observance or non-performance by the Tenant of any of its other obligations under

this Agreement then the Landlord shall be entitled forthwith to terminate the tenancy and that without prejudice to the Landlord's rights, claims and remedies for the Rent, interest, damages and expenses.

8.4 The Tenant agrees that its liability for the Rent and for the performance of the Tenant's whole obligations under this Agreement shall subsist, unless otherwise agreed by the Landlord in writing as continuing obligations, until the latest of the following dates:

8.4.1 the end of the Term;

8.4.2 the Termination Date;

8.4.3 the date of the Tenant's removing from and giving the Landlord vacant possession of the Premises and restoring the items on the Inventory to the Landlord.

9. Where the context so admits:

9.1 the 'Landlord' includes the persons for the time being the Owners of the Property;

9.2 the 'Tenant' includes any persons permitted to derive title from the Tenant;

9.3 the 'Property' includes any part or parts of the Property and all of the Landlord's fixtures and fittings at or upon the Property;

9.4 the 'Term' shall mean the period stated in the particulars overleaf or any shorter or longer period in the event of an earlier termination or an extension or holding over respectively;

9.4 the 'Termination Date' shall mean the date given by the Landlord in the Termination Notice (Section 33 Notice) and Notice to Quit being the date by which the tenant is required to leave the Property or alternatively the date given by the Tenant in his written Notice of Termination being the date the Tenant intends to leave the Property;

9.5 all references to 'he', 'him' and 'his' shall be taken to include 'she', 'her' and 'hers'.

10. All references to the singular shall include the plural and vice versa and any obligations or liabilities of more than one person shall be joint and several and an obligation on the part of a party shall include an obligation not to allow or permit the breach of that obligation.

11. This Agreement will be governed by and construed in accordance with the Law of Scotland and the parties submit to the jurisdiction of the Scottish Courts.

Insert here any additional terms you would like incorporated into the Agreement.	Additional provisions (if any)	_____

Landlord signs here	Landlord's signature _____
Witness (if any) signs here	Witness's signature _____
All tenants to sign here	Tenant's signature(s) _____
Witness (if any) to sign here	Witness's signature _____
Guarantor to sign here (if any)	Guarantor's signature _____
Witness to sign here	Witness's signature _____

SCOTLAND

LANDLORDS' NOTICE TO TERMINATE

SHORT ASSURED TENANCY

FROM:
LANDLORDS
_____ (name and address)
_____
_____

TO:
TENANT
_____ (name and address)
_____
_____

DATE: _____

PROPERTY: _____
_____

The above Landlords hereby give formal notice to the above Tenant under Section 33 of the Housing (Scotland) Act 1988 of their intention to bring the Tenant's tenancy to an end and recover possession of the above property currently occupied by the Tenant.

In terms of Section 33 of the aforementioned Act the Tenant must receive at least two months notice of the Landlords' intention to recover possession. Please therefore take note that you require to vacate the premises no later than _____. (insert date)

NOTE
This Notice to Terminate and Notice to Quit overleaf should both be completed and sent to the Tenant at least two months before the end of the tenancy.

133

SCOTLAND

SHORT ASSURED TENANCY NOTICE TO QUIT

NOTICE OF REMOVAL UNDER SECTION 37
OF THE SHERIFF COURTS (SCOTLAND) ACT 1907

FROM:
LANDLORDS _____ (name and address)
_____
_____
_____

TO:
TENANT _____ (name and address)
_____
_____
_____

DATE: _____

PROPERTY: _____
_____

The above Landlords hereby give notice to the above Tenant that the Tenant is required to remove from the above property at the _____day of _____ in terms (insert dates) of Lease between the Landlords and the Tenant dated _____.

The undernoted schedule which is incorporated herein complies with the Assured Tenancies (Notice to Quit Prescribed Information) (Scotland) Regulations 1988.

SCHEDULE

1. Even after the Notice to Quit has run out, before the tenant can be lawfully evicted, the landlord must get an Order for Possession from the Court.

2. If the Landlord issues a Notice to Quit but does not seek to gain possession of the Property in question the contractual assured tenancy which has been terminated will be replaced by a Statutory Assured Tenancy. In such circumstances the Landlord may propose new terms for the tenancy and may seek an adjustment in rent at annual intervals thereafter.

3. If a tenant does not know what kind of tenancy he has or is otherwise unsure of his rights he can obtain advice from a Solicitor. Help with all or part of the cost of legal advice and assistance can be available under the Legal Aid Legislation. A tenant can also seek help from a Citizens Advice Bureau or Housing Advisory Centre.

ENGLAND & WALES and SCOTLAND

HOUSEHOLD INVENTORY

Re _____ (the Property)

Living Room

No.	Item	Comment	In	Out	No.	Item	Comment	In	Out
	Armchair					Sofa			
	Ashtray					Table			
	Chairs					Table lamp			
	Coffee table					Telephone			
	Curtains					Television			
	Cushions					Vase			
	Doors					Video			
	Floor covering					Wall clock			
	Framed picture					Walls			
	Stereo system					Windows			
	Mirror								
	Net curtains								
	Plant								
	Rug								

Kitchen / Dining Room

No.	Item	Comment	In	Out	No.	Item	Comment	In	Out
	Apron					Potato peeler			
	Baking tray					Pudding/Soup dishes			
	Bottle opener					Pyrex dish			
	Bread bin					Roasting dish			
	Carving knives					Rolling pin			
	Casserole dish					Salt & pepper pots			
	Cheese grater					Saucepans			
	Chopping board					Scales			
	Coffee pot					Serving dishes			
	Corkscrew					Side plates			
	Cups					Sieve			
	Dessert spoons					Soup spoons			
	Dinner plates					Spatula			
	Dishwasher					Storage jars			
	Doors					Sugar jug			
	Draining board					Swing bin			
	Egg cups					Table			
	Floor covering					Tablecloth			
	Forks					Table mats			
	Fridge/Freezer					Teapot			
	Fruit bowl					Teaspoons			
	Frying pans					Tea towels			
	Garlic crusher					Tin opener			
	Glasses					Toaster			
	Kettle					Tray			
	Knives					Walls			
	Liquidiser					Washing machine			
	Measuring jug					Washing up bowl			
	Microwave					Windows			
	Milk jug					Wok			
	Mugs					Wooden spoons			
	Mug tree								
	Net curtains								
	Oven & Hob								
	Pie dishes								

135

Storage Cupboard

No.	Item	Comment	In	Out	No.	Item	Comment	In	Out
	Broom					Mop			
	Bucket					Vacuum cleaner			
	Clothes horse								
	Dustpan & brush								
	Iron								
	Ironing board								

Hall

No.	Item	Comment	In	Out	No.	Item	Comment	In	Out
	Coat stand					Net curtains			
	Doors					Walls			
	Floor covering					Windows			
	Framed picture								

Bedroom One

No.	Item	Comment	In	Out	No.	Item	Comment	In	Out
	Blankets					Net curtains			
	Bed sheets					Pillows			
	Chair					Pillowcases			
	Chest of drawers					Side table			
	Curtains					Single bed			
	Doors					Table mirror			
	Double bed					Wall mirror			
	Dressing table					Walls			
	Duvet					Wardrobe			
	Duvet cover					Windows			
	Floor covering								
	Framed picture								
	Lamp								
	Mattress cover								

Bedroom Two

No.	Item	Comment	In	Out	No.	Item	Comment	In	Out
	Blankets					Net curtains			
	Bed sheets					Pillows			
	Chair					Pillowcases			
	Chest of drawers					Side table			
	Curtains					Single bed			
	Doors					Table mirror			
	Double bed					Wall mirror			
	Dressing table					Walls			
	Duvet					Wardrobe			
	Duvet cover					Windows			
	Floor covering								
	Framed picture								
	Lamp								
	Mattress cover								

Bedroom Three

No.	Item	Comment	In	Out	No.	Item	Comment	In	Out
	Blankets					Net curtains			
	Bed sheets					Pillows			
	Chair					Pillowcases			
	Chest of drawers					Side table			
	Curtains					Single bed			
	Doors					Table mirror			
	Double bed					Wall mirror			
	Dressing table					Walls			
	Duvet					Wardrobe			
	Duvet cover					Windows			
	Floor covering								
	Framed picture								
	Lamp								
	Mattress cover								

Bedroom Four

No.	Item	Comment	In	Out	No.	Item	Comment	In	Out
	Blankets					Net curtains			
	Bed sheets					Pillows			
	Chair					Pillowcases			
	Chest of drawers					Side table			
	Curtains					Single bed			
	Doors					Table mirror			
	Double bed					Wall mirror			
	Dressing table					Walls			
	Duvet					Wardrobe			
	Duvet cover					Windows			
	Floor covering								
	Framed picture								
	Lamp								
	Mattress cover								

Bathroom

No.	Item	Comment	In	Out	No.	Item	Comment	In	Out
	Basket					Wall mirror			
	Doors					Walls			
	Floor covering					Windows			
	Floor mat					Wooden chair			
	Lavatory brush								
	Net curtains								
	Shower curtain								
	Soap dish								
	Towels								

Signed _____   _____

(Landlord)   (Tenant)

137

Roger Sproston

STRAIGHTFORWARD GUIDES

Straightforward guides are published through Straightforward Publishing. Straightforward Publishing produces a range of guides, under the imprint Straightforward Guides, Easyway Guides and Key advice Guides plus Emerald Guides. We have over 95 titles covering law, business, personal development, careers, Information technology and general titles.

If you would like to know more about our range of books or would like to know more about Straightforward Guides, please contact us through our web site at:

www.straightforwardco.co.uk
e-mail info@straighforwardco.co.uk